I WRITE THE
YAWNING VOID

I WRITE THE YAWNING VOID

SELECTED ESSAYS OF SINDIWE MAGONA

Compiled and edited by Renée Schatteman

WITS UNIVERSITY PRESS

Published in South Africa by:
Wits University Press
1 Jan Smuts Avenue
Johannesburg 2001

www.witspress.co.za

First published 2023

http://dx.doi.org.10.18772/22023078189

978-1-77614-818-9 (Paperback)
978-1-77614-819-6 (Hardback)
978-1-77614-820-2 (Web PDF)
978-1-77614-821-9 (EPUB)

This publication is peer reviewed following international best practice standards for academic and scholarly books.

Project manager: Alison Paulin
Copyeditor: Lynda Gilfillan
Proofreader: Alison Paulin
Indexer: Marlene Burger
Cover design: Ayanda Phasha
Typeset in 11 point A Caslon Pro

To all my children,
Flesh and spiritual:
Thank you
For making me the mother I am.

CONTENTS

ACKNOWLEDGEMENTS AND PERMISSIONS

The author and editor acknowledge with gratitude permission to reprint, in edited and in some cases substantially revised form, material by the author published previously as indicated below.

Chapter 1: 'The Scars of Umlungu' was first published in *New Internationalist* 230 (April), 1992. It can be found online at https://newint.org/features/1992/04/05/scars.

Chapter 2: 'Clawing at Stones' was first published in *The Spirit of Writing: Classic and Contemporary Essays Celebrating the Writing Life*, edited by Mark Robert Waldman (New York: Jeremy P. Tarcher/Putman, 2001), 7–13.

Chapter 3: 'Finding My Way Home' is a substantially revised version, which first appeared in the magazine *Fairlady* in June 2006.

Chapter 4: 'It is in the Blood: Trauma and Memory in the South African Novel' was first published in *Trauma, Memory, and Narrative in the Contemporary South African Novel* (Cross Cultures 153), edited by Ewald Mengel and Michaela Borzaga (Leiden: Brill, 2012), 93–105. It is included here with permission from Brill.

Chapter 9: 'Why I Wrote My Autobiographies' is a substantially revised version, which was first published as 'The Impact of Colonialism and Postcolonialism on Women's Writing' in *Five Points: A Journal of Literature and Arts* no. 19.1 (Winter), 2018: 102–106.

Chapter 11: 'Why I Wrote *Beauty's Gift*' was first published as the Introduction to *Beauty's Gift* (Johannesburg: Pan Macmillan, 2018), 1–39. This version has been shortened and revised.

FOREWORD

I Write the Yawning Void is a collection of essays by the celebrated South African writer, storyteller and activist, Sindiwe Magona. Known for her many contributions to a wide range of literary genres (autobiographies, short stories, plays, novels, poems, biographies and children's books), she has received less attention for the essays she has penned over the course of her career. Magona began to engage in expository writing with an article for the *New Internationalist* magazine in 1992, two years after she published her first full-length work, the autobiography *To My Children's Children*. She went on to publish other short prose pieces in this journal and in a variety of other venues, even as she was taking on one literary genre after another and establishing a name for herself in South African letters.

Today, Magona is well recognised as one of the country's most significant writers and a seminal figure in South African women's writing. She has received more than twenty awards since she began writing – most notably, the Xhosa Heroes Award in 1997 (which recognises those who work to uplift their communities); the Proclamation Award from New York State in 2003 (for her artistic work on the issues of HIV and Aids); the South African Molteno Gold Medal in 2007 (for her role in promoting isiXhosa); the Italian Premio Grinzane Terre D'Otrantro in 2007 (for writing that promotes dialogue between people); the Presidential Order of Ikhamanga in

2011 for outstanding achievement in literature and playwriting (the highest such award in South Africa); the Mbokodo Award for Creative Writing in 2012 (which she shared with Nobel Laureate Nadine Gordimer); as well as the English Academy of Southern Africa Gold Medal Award in 2016 and the André Brink Award in 2018, both of which pay tribute to her oeuvre. In addition, Magona has been awarded four honorary doctorates (from Hartwick College in the USA and also from Rhodes University, Nelson Mandela University and Fort Hare University in South Africa), and she completed a PhD in Creative Writing at the University of the Western Cape in 2022. In addition, she is among the list of 'Living Legends', a programme created by the South African Government's Department of Arts and Culture.

Given Magona's stature as a revered spokesperson for women and for marginalised people in general, a publication which gathers her most important essays into a single collection is both fitting and timely. The essays serve as critically important supplements to her fiction, even as they stand alone as important reflections on life and culture in South Africa. They merit critical attention because of the way in which they illustrate the power of her voice as conveyed through the direct reflection that essay writing affords.

Magona's various prose pieces run the range from formal to informal and take a variety of forms: recollections from personal life, observations of societal trends, comments on South Africa's literary landscape, and passionate arguments about the causes of and possible remedies for South Africa's social ills. The 14 pieces collected here give particular emphasis to her thoughts on writing: how she came to it, what she feels about the state of writing and language use in South Africa today, and why she was inspired to write her various pieces. A few of the essays included here do not explicitly address writing, but they serve as especially poignant examples of the most prominent features of Magona's aesthetics: her use of deeply embedded metaphors, her activist leanings, and her willingness to assume and defend unpopular opinions. These elements combine in these works to produce powerful prose that addresses what Magona calls 'South Africa's yawning void'.

Ever since she began publishing over thirty years ago, Magona's fictional works have been lauded for the way they capture the richness of the country's cultural context while also asserting insightful and often pointed critique, and these traits are abundantly apparent in her essays as well. Likewise, the central beliefs that underpin her fiction – the importance of women and women's lives, the dignity and equal value of all human beings, the inherent evil of race hate, the critical need for education, and so on – also form the foundation of her prose pieces. Similarly, in her essays, she assumes the role that she has adopted elsewhere – of a truthteller who challenges readers by shedding new light on social perversions that they have become accustomed to and accepted as normal. Magona employs irony as an essential tool for exposing the contradictions that tear at the fabric of everyday life. A writer needs to trade in uncomfortable truths, she asserts in a 2018 interview, because

> the contrast between rhetoric and reality is the ugly reality of most of our lives – be it in education, religion, or politics … Human beings seem, certainly in my country, to walk through life with eyes half closed for fear of ever seeing the reality they live, must live.[1]

But while Magona's fiction and her prose share common themes and purposes, her essays stand apart from her other genres in important ways. The essay has a distinctive form that is particularly suited to a writer like Magona, who is both a gifted storyteller and an outspoken social critic, and to a context like South Africa, which still struggles with the many tensions and paradoxes it inherited from a history of racial separation and repressive rule.

Because the essay is a more direct form of expression than other genres, Magona considers it to be 'the most honest way of presenting yourself'[2] and a fitting vehicle for conveying the truths she is eager to get down on paper at this point in her career. The essays provide a glimpse into a writer's mind at work, tracing her process of coming to an understanding about the topics that demand her attention while also showcasing her persistent sense of optimism, something that is more muted in her fiction. Magona invariably insists that society's greatest obstacles can be overcome if people commit to identifying the root of a social ill, expressing outrage over its effects on human lives, and finding practical solutions that can be achieved through collaborative effort. All the essays contained in this collection embody these imperatives, in one way or another.

Magona's prose work also needs to be considered in the context of the Xhosa literary tradition that she comes from. Xhosa intellectuals of the early twentieth century, such as Tiyo Soga, John Tengo Jabavu, Mpilo Walter Benson Rubusana, and S.E.K. Mqhayi, also tried their hands at different modes of writing, moving easily across genres and between fiction and non-fiction. S.E.K. Mqhayi unquestionably had the greatest impact on Magona's own writing and thinking, something she acknowledges quite frequently. Considered the father of South African poetry, Mqhayi also distinguished himself as an essayist, a biographer and autobiographer, a novelist, a critic, an editor, an historian, a linguist, and a translator, and thereby set an example of a writer unrestricted by the conventions that typically assign authors to specific categories. He was also considered a pioneer of indigenous languages for his work in standardising the grammar of isiXhosa. In this regard, his influence can be detected in Magona's English-language writing (which is heavily inflected with Xhosa syntax and often includes Xhosa words, phrases, or entire passages, sometimes translated and sometimes not) and her passionate views on mother tongue (which are in close alignment with Mqhayi's mission to dislodge the hegemony of English and champion the various indigenous languages of the South African people).

The translations for Xhosa words found in these essays are provided by Magona herself. For the non-Xhosa-speaking reader, a noteworthy feature of isiXhosa is that all nouns have prefixes that always start with a vowel, for example ama-, in- (amaXhosa, inqoma); when translated, there is no need to use the article ('the'), for example 'amaXhosa' means the Xhosa people, while 'isiXhosa' means the Xhosa language. When these words are used as adjectives, the prefix is elided.

Magona's essays should be viewed in light of the spate of single-authored essay collections from South African writers that have been published in recent years, such as Ian McCallum's *Ecological Intelligence: Rediscovering Ourselves in Nature* (2008); Njabulo Ndebele's *Fine Lines from the Box* (2011); Ferial Haffajee's *What If There Were No Whites in South Africa?* (2015); Pumla Dineo Gqola's *Reflecting Rogue: Inside the Mind of a Feminist* (2018); and Zoë Wicomb's *Race, Nation, Translation* (2018). The fact that there is a market for this specific genre suggests a hunger on the part of South African readers for sustained reflections by well-established literary intellectuals on the development of the nation over the past thirty years or so. Featuring pieces that were written over time and published in various venues and for various purposes, these collections accrue a significance and profundity as narratives of the collective experiences of independence and maturation which offer valuable analysis and insight into South Africa's successes, the challenges of the recent past, and its prospects for the future. Each collection has a unique take on the contemporary moment, reflective of the writer's accumulation of specific concerns. Gqola's autobiographical essays, for example, allow her to revisit the themes important to her other works – *What is Slavery to Me?* (2010); *Rape: A South African Nightmare* (2015); and *Female Fear Factory* (2021) – that revolve around women's safety, women's pleasure, and women's sense of themselves, but through a more personal, intimate lens. Wicomb's essays do not turn towards the personal but rather provide incisive analysis on race and culture in South Africa (echoing what is seen in her fictional works such as the 2000 *David's Story* and the 2006 *Playing in the Light*) as well as trenchant criticism of southern African literature and art. *Fine Lines* is not Ndebele's first collection of essays, for in 1991 the tremendously influential *Rediscovery of the Ordinary: South African Literature and Culture*[3] called for a new type of literary expression that was less preoccupied with protest and more focused on the complex ramifications of oppression on the interior world of the South African subject. His more recent essays are embroiled in a range of issues relevant to the post-apartheid context (such as corruption, HIV and Aids, higher education, leadership), and they also read against the grain by calling for objectivity and accountability instead of party loyalty and the persistent charge of racism levelled against whites in South African society.

Magona's prose writing resembles aspects of all three of these collections, especially Ndebele's, because her ideas parallel his emphasis on the mundane and on non-partisanship. But she also brings her own style of prose writing: extremely accessible, often highly personal, and representative of life at the margins. All the works in this collection are tied, in one way or another, to Magona's own life story of growing up in township poverty; falling into destitution as a single mother with three young children; and eventually transcending her circumstances to again join the workforce as a teacher, a translator at the United Nations Anti-Apartheid Radio Programmes, and a respected writer. Magona frequently draws upon this success narrative (which she insists was only possible with the help of many others) to inspire other South Africans to free themselves from the assumption that poverty is a permanent condition. In making such appeals, she presents the direct experience of someone who comes from the context about which she writes while simultaneously asserting interpretations of that experience as a writer removed from that context by her education and her life beyond the township. Her writing consequently combines a deep compassion for her subjects with a critical analysis of their human interactions – a marriage of the heart and the mind, so to speak. This dual focus makes her a figure admired by both the people she writes about and the scholars who seek to better understand South African culture. Her keen insights, based on the evidence of what she observes and records in detail, provide well-substantiated theories of how life was experienced under apartheid and is experienced now, in its aftermath.

In this manner, Magona's writing can be said to be responding to calls for work theorising black life that comes from within the community itself rather than being imposed from the outside. Ndebele made such a plea in his essay 'Turkish Tales and Some Thoughts on South African Fiction' (originally published in *Staffrider* in 1984 and later included in *Rediscovery of the Ordinary*), in which he lamented the lack of theory produced by black intellectuals and regretted that 'research and discussions about research tend to be confined to white liberal universities'.[4] This lacuna had damaging implications for the anti-apartheid movement, he further suggested, because it meant that 'any research of radical intent, which, by definition, has to emanate from, and its evaluation be situated in, the very African struggle as it evolves, has no organic relationship with the struggles. So it cannot enrich the struggle with the *immediate* resistance.'[5] In *Decolonizing Methodologies: Research and Indigenous Peoples* (1999), Linda Tuhiwai Smith similarly argues that indigenous people were often oppressed by the research done on them because 'most of the theorizing has been driven by anthropological approaches'.[6] Although she is writing about this topic from a New Zealand context, she insists upon the value of self-generated theory work for all indigenous communities. She writes, 'It enables us to make assumptions and predictions about the world in which we live. It contains within it a method for selecting and arranging, for prioritising and legitimating what we see and do. Theory enables us to deal with the contradictions and uncertainties. Perhaps more significantly it gives us space to play, to strategise, to take greater control over our lives'.[7] Smith's description of the uses of theory resonates on multiple levels throughout Magona's oeuvre and within this collection of essays.

I Write the Yawning Void comprises 16 pieces, including the introduction and conclusion, six of which were previously published and ten of which were unpublished, delivered as speeches over the past five years, or written very recently for this collection. (The fact that nearly two thirds of the pieces in this collection represent material which has not yet appeared in print makes this work especially significant as an addition to Magona's oeuvre.) With the exception of the introductory and concluding essays, the pieces are clustered into three sections: Coming into Writing; Writing about Pressing Issues; and Writing about My Writing.

Part 1, which features four previously published essays, represents the earliest period covered by the collection. These pieces examine what initially drove Magona to writing and what keeps her engaged in the craft and as prolific as ever, even after three decades. Though not the first essay, 'Clawing at Stones' (2001) tells the story of how she became a writer, despite there being only a handful of black female writers in the country who had preceded her, while 'Finding My Way Home' (2006) recounts how she returned to South Africa after her retirement from the United Nations, so as to be on the ground (rather than observing from a distance) when writing about issues of the day. These essays suggest that Magona's reasons for writing have matured and expanded over time, from merely wanting to leave a record for future generations to striving to inspire her contemporary readers to take the action required to gain control of their lives.

Magona's powerful essay 'It is in the Blood: Trauma and Memory in the South African Novel' (2012) is also included in this section because it digs deeper into an analysis of her own writing (and the work of other South African writers) by drawing attention to the inescapable impact of colonialism and apartheid on the South African psyche. She writes that the clash of cultures initiated by colonial conquest ended in the complete domination of the subjugated people, which has had extremely disruptive and long-lasting effects. Drawing attention to the way that all South Africans were damaged in one way or another by apartheid, Magona creates an extremely useful construct for understanding the inability of writers from her country to get beyond the trauma of the past.

The first essay in Part 1 (Coming into Writing), entitled 'The Scars of *Umlungu*' (1992), stands apart from these other works in that it does not explicitly mention writing at all. It is included here nonetheless because it was Magona's published essay and because it provides a piquant example of one of the qualities that distinguishes her work from that of other writers: namely, her profound use of metaphor. Her multivalent use of metaphor is also apparent in the aforementioned titles 'Clawing at Stones' and 'It is in the Blood' (the first of which is used to describe the hardships Magona's father faced in his work at the mines as well as the pain she experienced in mining her own recollections to write about the humiliations imposed on African people under apartheid, and the second of which refers to both the debilitating trauma South Africans have inherited from the past and the dangerous inclination towards violence that apartheid also bequeathed its citizens).

'The Scars of *Umlungu*' takes metaphor even further in likening the faces of African women, pockmarked by skin-lightening creams popular during the apartheid period, to the scarred African landscape. With this analogy, Magona signals her interest in 'ecofeminism' and the parallels it establishes 'between man's millennial attempts to subdue nature and women', as argued by critic Dianne Shober.[8]

The move to metaphor that is so intrinsic to Magona's writing is likely a carry-over from her mother tongue, isiXhosa, which encourages the technique of describing something with words describing something else, as illustrated in the language's investment in proverbs (which, in essence, function as extended metaphors). Magona's essays also feature other elements reflecting the care she takes with the sound and the feel of language in her writing: her frequent injection of isiXhosa into her writing; her easy slippages between prose and poetry; and her tendency to pile on details when describing a phenomenon, which results in writing thick with cultural referencing. All these factors culminate in a texture and a cadence that is uniquely Magona's.

Part 2, entitled 'Writing about Pressing Issues', speaks to social problems that Magona has taken on (both in her writing and in her public engagements) with the fiery determination of an optimist who believes in the power of collective action to right (or, at least, minimise) social wrongs. The problems addressed in these essays – HIV and Aids, poverty, the lack of respect for indigenous languages, and racial tensions – collectively represent much of what hinders South Africa from achieving the vision of the 'rainbow nation' promoted at the time of its transition to democracy.

Part 2 also showcases a second aspect of Magona's literary endeavours: her willingness to blur the line that typically divides imaginative writing from activism. Because these two types of work rely upon opposing instincts (ambiguity and open-endedness in the case of the first, and surety and single-mindedness in the case of the second), fiction writers usually avoid writing that overtly prescribes actions readers should take in response to a certain situation. Magona bends that rule in her post-apartheid fiction, especially in the novel *Beauty's Gift* and her other literature about HIV and Aids, which impresses upon readers the need for immediate action to stem the shocking tide of infections that has caused South Africa to become the epicentre of the global Aids crisis. But the essay is a more flexible genre which can more readily accommodate different impulses, and Magona takes full advantage of that to turn these essays into passionate appeals that seek to galvanise readers into action.

'Address at the Funeral of a Young Woman' (previously unpublished) expresses Magona's outrage about the steady stream of funerals taking place in the country and the stigma and silence that have allowed for the rapid acceleration of Aids-related deaths. She calls out all those responsible for the crisis, especially men who endanger the lives of women through infidelity and sexual violence, and advocates for adults to assume their responsibility in protecting the young from harm, and for all South Africans to place self-preservation above everything in this moment of crisis.

'Do Not Choose Poverty' (previously unpublished) addresses the social ill that underlies all the problems that bedevil South Africa, and deconstructs the belief that poverty is a stranglehold that necessarily keeps people from achieving success in their lives. Drawing upon her own experience as an example, Magona maps out the steps that individuals can take to escape poverty, if they begin to identify the practical measures needed to inch their way towards their personal goals. Taking the risk of being labelled an extreme conservative who holds poor people responsible for their unfortunate circumstances, Magona speaks directly to the many South Africans who are financially oppressed and presents her own life struggle in detail, thereby redefining the discourse around poverty to prioritise agency over victimhood.

'Cry, the Beloved Language' (previously unpublished) explores the state of mother-tongue usage in South Africa, which may appear an insignificant issue to many but to Magona is a problem with tremendous implications. Deeply concerned about the antagonism towards African languages, Magona concludes that South Africans are doing damage to themselves when they distance themselves from their indigenous languages. Her central assumption is that mother-tongue language is a crucial component of self-identification, and that the neglect of the one will necessarily contribute to the erosion of the other. This essay illuminates Magona's distinctive stance on the language debate in African literature that she has staked out over the course of her career. As a writer who has written most of her works in English (with the exception of her children's literature) while also championing indigenous languages and promoting writing in isiXhosa, she effectively merges the priorities advanced by Chinua Achebe (who promoted the concept of writing in an Africanised English) with those articulated by Ngũgĩ wa Thiong'o (who insisted that mother-tongue language use was the only means of capturing an authentic expression).

The final essay in this section is by far her most contentious: 'We Are All Racists!' (previously unpublished). In it, Magona enters the charged arena of race and upends assumed truths by redefining the meaning of racism and challenging people to focus more on overcoming the damaging and long-lasting effects of racial discrimination (whether conveyed through action or word) than on accusing one another of racism. Her position is not meant to diminish the gravity of the suffering caused by the racial hierarchies of the past but rather to offer practical suggestions for getting beyond the preoccupation with and misunderstandings about race in the present.

Magona's essays in Part 3 (Writing about My Writing) are very illuminating when read alongside her literature, for in each of them she explains the genesis of a text, the process of writing it, and (sometimes) its reception. But these pieces can also be read independently as engaging reflections upon her life and also piercing commentaries on social ills. In addition, they showcase one final element of Magona's aesthetics: her willingness to say out loud truths that many others would rather have left unsaid.

The uncomfortable truth embedded in 'Why I Wrote My Autobiographies' (2018) is Magona's admission about how severely she was impacted by the debilitating environment of her upbringing. The essay highlights what it took to overcome apartheid's assumption of black inferiority enough to be able to put pen to paper. What finally enabled her to transcend her feelings of insignificance was her awareness, gained during her involvement in interracial anti-apartheid efforts, that whites generally did not understand the impact on the non-white population of the policies enacted in their name, and that she consequently had important things to say.

'Why I Wrote *Mother to Mother*' (previously unpublished) recounts the story of how Magona came to write about the death of Amy Biehl – an American Fulbright scholar who was stabbed to death in 1993 by a group of youths engaged in an anti-apartheid protest – after her discovery that the mother of one of the accused killers was a childhood friend. That knowledge humanised the killer for Magona and gave her the courage to write a novel that exposes the deep-seated and lingering issue of black resentment towards whites, a reality covered over in the Truth and Reconciliation Commission hearings of the late 1990s.

'Why I Wrote *Beauty's Gift*', a 2019 essay, explores the heart-wrenching circumstances caused by HIV and Aids that prompted Magona to become one of the few writers producing work directly addressing the epidemic raging in her country (*Beauty's Gift* was published in 2008). This essay is intertwined with the earlier essay 'Address at the Funeral of a Young Woman', which originated in a speech she had delivered at the graveside of a family friend.

That event, she recounts in this essay, was the turning point that enabled her to overcome her fear and create a novel about the suffering being inflicted upon the whole country by the virus and the factors that enabled it – namely, the neglect of the government, the sexual irresponsibility of men, and societal acceptance of these shortcomings.

Chasing the Tails of My Father's Cattle (2015) and *When the Village Sleeps* (2021) are Magona's most recent novels, one about the status of women in rural South Africa and the other about the endangerment of township children in the present moment. Magona's previously unpublished essays about these works explain the disturbing realities that she fictionalises in each. In the case of the first novel, this involves the diminished sense of trustworthiness and honour among South African men, while in the second this materialises through questions the text raises about the ethics and the efficacy of the government's child support grant. Both challenge principles that form the bedrock of modern South African society: the protection of male entitlement and assumed dependency on governmental assistance.

In the final essay of this section, 'Why I Write Children's Books' (previously unpublished), Magona explores the many factors that motivated her to write more than 130 children's books, the majority in isiXhosa: to invite children into the magic of stories; to tap into the sense of wonder that is inherent in children; to promote mother tongue in the education of children; and to help children transcend South Africa's troubled past through the healing power of narrative. All these concerns tap into Magona's deep-seated belief that children are central to the future of the nation and that many more resources should be devoted to ensuring that they flourish.

When the essays are taken together, they bring to life the various facets that feed into Magona's analytical processes: her personal history, her self-awareness, her deepest convictions, her keen sense of people and of human motivation, her love for her country, her despair at its current state, her hope for its betterment, and the belief in her ability to activate change. And while these pieces echo the aesthetics found in her fiction, especially her talent for telling an engaging story, they have a particular appeal in their demonstration of Magona's mastery of yet another literary genre. *I Write the Yawning Void* makes an important contribution to Magona's vast corpus, one that charts her thinking across the three decades of her writing career and provides a record of the touchpoints in South African society and culture under apartheid, during the transition years, and in the post-apartheid period.

Renée Schatteman
Compiler and editor, *I Write the Yawning Void*

INTRODUCTION
WRITING SOUTH AFRICA'S YAWNING VOID

I CAN'T BELIEVE I have been writing for more than three decades. However, even my feeble maths tells me that 33 years ago, *To My Children's Children*, announced – to those interested in such matters – the arrival of a new writer named Sindiwe Magona: this book was published by David Philip Publishers in 1990.

To reflect on what writing has meant, and continues to mean, to me is, therefore, to go back a long, a very long time. At the start of this rollercoaster journey, let me reiterate, there was a much-surprised person. I was surprised at what I had somehow managed to do – write a book. Even more surprised that a publisher had not only wanted to publish it, but had gone ahead and done just that. Then, as though that were not miracle enough to kill a person, guess what? There were people who bought the book, read the book – from page one to the very last page – and didn't try and find me and laugh at me or, worse still, throw rotten eggs at me. No, they read the book, read it like any normal book. So, the whole thing had not just been a figment of my imagination. How could that be? The whole world shared in my wild, wild dream, my fantasy. It had to be real, then. I had written a book. And the book was published by a reputable publisher.

The book went on to garner great reviews. And thirty years later, it is still in print! Sindiwe Magona – author. But what did this mean to me, then? What does it mean today? What inspired me to write that book in the first place, and what has inspired me to keep at it, keep on writing, ever since? The following poem, found in my collection, *Please, Take Photographs* (2009), provides some answers to these questions:

Statement

I come to writing with no great learning
Except my life and the life of the people
Of whom I am a part. For centuries,
Others have written about us
I write to change that
Instead of moaning about it.
I write so that children who look like me
In my country,
And my people, dispersed
Throughout the world,
May see someone who looks like them
Do this thing that has for so long
Not belonged to us.
I write so that the tale of the hunt
May be heard also, from the mouth of
The hunted, the hated of this world,
For only then, will that story
Be anywhere near complete ...[1]

I look at my writing, look at what provokes it. I use the word 'provoke' for, strangely, my writing seems to come out of anger, disgust, disappointment, sadness or grief; it is provoked by a deep dissatisfaction with some aspect of the life I witness all around me, a life gone all awry. Provoked, then, not inspired ... at least not as far as the subject matter is concerned. Let us look at the poem above and ask, 'What provoked that?'

The answer to that question – not only about the poem but most, if not all, of the writing I have done – is the content of this volume of essays. *I Write the Yawning Void* is a book of essays about the writing I have done – the why and wherefore of it. I hope to take the reader through my writing or the reason/s behind the writing of each novel, story, play, poem or essay. The interested reader, I dare say, will discover one or another of the sentiments mentioned above. Notice that joy doesn't make me burst into song – except, now that I think of it, in poetry. Yes, in poetry I do occasionally write on some of the more joyous of life's events, people and circumstances. But in my novels, short stories, and even in my essays, I seem to ponder over the – sadly – rich vein of human misery to bring to light situations that are void of human fulfilment.

A void is different things to different people. Toni Morrison is commonly known to have said that she writes the books she wants to read – now, there's a void. I write the books I wish were not necessary – books for which there was no need. However, to my way of seeing the world, each book is an injunction to some, if not all, members of society to stop doing what they should not have done or, depending on the matter that provoked the writing of the book, to do what they ought to have done: acts of commission or omission. The warnings, of course, do not apply to factual writing such as biography, which deals with lived history. Nor would cookbooks, I suppose, fall under this category.

That first book, *To My Children's Children* (1990), as well as the sequel, *Forced to Grow* (1992) – both autobiographies, worked to fill the strange void of absence. Complete absence of me and people like me from books. Not as I know myself. Not as I knew people among whom I lived. When there were women who looked anything like me, my mother, grandmother, aunt or neighbour – an African or 'Bantu' in apartheid terminology – they were sure to be smiling maids in uniform, out at the park minding white children or pushing a pram on the pavement, with a white baby in the pram. It took me a long, very long time to see that absence. Amazing what one gets used to, accepts as the norm. But then, when that is all one has ever seen, why would the void have been noticeable? You only miss something to which you are accustomed. As the poem at the beginning of this essay explains, and the title of the book spells out, I write to tell a story – my story. My people's story. History as it is lived.

But then, after that first book, more books followed. And more. And more. More, hopefully, will follow still. The void yawns, still. And it wears many, many faces – similar or very different faces. Absence or cancellation; othering in all its different guises; poverty; greed and dreadfully incompetent governance; oppression; violence and violation of the rights of humans, animals, living things and the environment; and so on and so on ... the violation of Life and the right to life for all.

Why, you ask, do I persist in writing the yawning void? Believe it or not, I don't plumb these dark corners of the human heart because I love unhappiness or evil – No! I go there because, despite abundant evidence to the contrary, I believe human beings were meant to be, could be, and deserve to be abundantly happy! So, yes, my writings are almost always elicited by the sadder, rather than happier, events in life. However, I do become inspired writing them – inspired by what my words might do, the work they might accomplish. So, in a way, my books, at least to my way of seeing things, should do the work I am too timid, cowardly, unwilling to do, or incapable of doing up front.

Writing the void, therefore, is my interrogation and/or pursuit of the state of happiness that eludes most of us mere mortals, since more and more of us have given up on the idea of happiness or the abundance of a simple life, or living a stress-free life, satisfied, uncluttered; respectful, and assuming respect. A world in which all people respect themselves, respect others, and respect the generous and bountiful environment that is the very breath of life.

Respect for Self.

Respect for the Other.

Respect for the Environment.

That is my ideal, but then there is the void – the gap; the empty space; the unoccupied position … what is absent, not there … when it should be. So, I suppose one could say I write from a gnawing hunger for things we dream of but lack the imagination or courage to work hard enough to make happen. The future we all want, for which we wait – and wait – and wait … little realising it is waiting for us to birth it, bring it into being.

And what might provoke, instantly or otherwise, the onset of a book or essay is nothing I understand. Reading a book, magazine or newspaper; news on radio or television; a word or words someone says during a conversation or at a meeting – sparks fly in my mind instantly, in a flash, or an ember softly falls onto the seemingly asleep fire in my heart. Later – hours, days, or much later – a sizzling grows and grows and, suddenly, there is a flare.

I may disregard or want to disregard the spark, tell myself I should not take everything to heart, but, if it is going to burst into writing, it will. There is no mightier conflagration than an idea that lights up in a writer's mind. It will goad and goad and goad till she answers the call – even if that writing ends up on the scrap pile or the growing stack of 'to be submitted' or 'not yet published', the pile of a writer's unanswered outpourings, waiting still … But whatever kindled the writing is, to the writer, something that warrants the eye of the nation, if not that of the world. It has been said that writers see more clearly than others in society. If this is the gift that drives my writing, I welcome it, though I would never have bought it for myself had I had the option. It is not always a blessing to see what others do not see; fear for a future they do not fear, as their eyes do not perceive the steps leading to the horror the writer sees at the step they are about to take.

Stop!

One genre of writing which enables me to address these dangers and speak to the void more directly is the essay, a type of writing that I have always appreciated, and so I close this essay with a reflection on this form. I was hugely surprised when, soon after *To My Children's Children* was published in 1990, I received requests for articles, or essays. Not a book of essays such as the one you're wading through now, but a single essay. The requests usually came from a magazine or a newspaper, although I was also asked to contribute an essay to a collection. I accepted the first request with alacrity. I have always enjoyed expository writing. As a child in primary school, if the teacher decided to select an essay (or composition, as we then called it) to read to the class, ten out of ten times, that essay would be mine. That says a lot when my classmates included the likes of the late Sidney Zola Skweyiva – a huge brain with whom I fought for first position in all the exams.[2] But when it came to language – isiXhosa or English – I was one up on him.

The only reason I have not become exclusively or a more prolific writer of essays is that, from the word go I was told 'Essays don't sell!' That, in my humble opinion, is a pity. So, I mainly wrote essays only when requested, and one request was followed by another and another. Sometimes, however, I would write an essay simply because I felt like it. There is something emotionally satisfying, for me, in putting my thoughts down with no consideration of fitting this into that. An essay is a stand-alone piece of writing – more like a short story than a novel. The writer says what she has to say on a specific topic and, within a short space of time, it's done!

One would think, therefore, that with this clear advantage over longer pieces, essays would be the preferred form – of both the writer and the reader. This was, indeed, once the case, as shown by the abundance of books of essays where a writer might have published thirty or forty or more essays in a single volume. But nowadays, that would be a hard thing to find. What we more frequently come across is a volume containing essays from several contributors. While the variety of voices, styles and subject matter may make for interesting reading, it is a shame to be deprived of the reach and expanse of an individual essayist; to experience the insights, delights, likes and aversions a particular writer may express or share through her essays.

The idea that publishers are not keen on essays because readers are not keen on reading essays persists in my mind, and persists in bothering me. Why is this so? Why has the essay fallen into disfavour, or gone out of fashion? I am told that schools have stopped teaching the form. For goodness' sake, why has this happened, and why have we, society at large, allowed it to happen?

But perhaps a revival is afoot. Pumla Dineo Gqola has delighted us with *Reflecting Rogue: Inside the Mind of an African Feminist*. Her essays display mind- and heart-piercing honesty. Ferial Haffajee offers a similarly provocative collection in *What If There Were No Whites in South Africa?*, while Njabulo Ndebele proves himself evergreen with his *Fine Lines from the Box* and Ian McCallum gets us to look at the world anew in *Ecological Intelligence: Rediscovering Ourselves in Nature*. This is to name but a few collections of essays that speak of today's issues; relevant and delightfully insightful, they are a treasure trove.

Please, dear publishers, let us have more of these delights. And dear fellow writers, more and more and more essays, please! I beg you all, let us not allow this once-favoured genre to die. See how the comedian has risen in popularity. What does he do? Provoke his audience into new awareness of that which it already knows. Make people take a fresh look at themselves and laugh at what they have seen or heard or read: the known dressed in iridescent colours of penetrating humour. We can do the same with our essays.

What are we waiting for, fellow writers? We all know that there is enough material out there for both the hilarious and the serious essay. Let's get on with it! We don't need permission or degrees or anything else to write essays. We can't wait till someone wakes up to what the essay can deliver and puts it back into the school curriculum before we've in fact written the essays. Let us write essays in defiance, if need be. But, write them, we must. Like all the other writing we do, we will get better and better at writing essays only when we write them – that is the one guarantee I can give regarding writing. As has often been said, practice makes perfect. This is surely the time to perfect a form that can so explicitly address the yawning void: the deep-seated hurt in all the peoples of this beautiful land. What is the nature of that hurt? What does the hurt really, deeply, mean?

In all the essays I have produced during my career, I have written for my fellow South Africans to help them see what they are missing, what is perhaps not clear to them. I write for my nation, our nation, the beloved country of South Africa. Yes, it is for you most of all, Beloved, that I write. I write about you, for you. All my wishes for the nation you have the potential to be – my highest hope, for you dearest, is that you will become that which you teeter on the brink of becoming. If only … if only you could be bold enough, courageous enough, fear-free enough to let go of your hideous past. Not forget it, no! But put it where it belongs, in the catacombs of yesterday, and gird your loins to do that which awaits your action: cleanse your wounds of the hurt of racism, discrimination, poverty, lack of education and all that smells of the rot of what was. That done, take up the new fight for the better-for-all tomorrow so that – with hate banished from our hearts, hurts healed, fear and fearfulness left behind – we all join hands and, together, meld this multicultural melange that we are into a joyous union. Why do we not hurry to be the envy of the whole world? To be the model, the example other nations follow? The ingredients are certainly here, we are here, coloured all hues of the human palette. I write for the vision that we are, can be, and will be!

If only!

PART I
COMING TO WRITING

The essays contained in this section were all previously published, as articles in journals or chapters in essay collections. They represent the earliest written work in this collection. In them, Sindiwe Magona examines how she came to writing; why she continues writing after three decades; and what she understands to be the challenges for writers in South Africa.

1.
THE SCARS OF *UMLUNGU*

Magona's earliest published piece of published prose, this essay appeared in the New Internationalist *volume 230 in April 1992. It provides a compelling example of Magona's ability to fashion unique and deeply embedded metaphors that she uses in her writing to convey large-scale experiences such as the colonial conquest of land and the accompanying destruction of the African way of life.*

MY PEOPLE HAVE their own ways of doing things. We have always had our ways of doing things. 'The ones scrubbed in hot water' could not see this when they came. They came – 'the ones with coloured eyes' – and found my people living worthwhile lives that were satisfying to them. But the newcomers saw only indolence, ignorance and superstition. They saw nothing commendable, nothing worth preserving, least of all emulating. For them, our being alive held no lessons whatsoever. It proved nothing. They had their ways. And, in their eyes, these were far, far superior to ours. So began the destruction of my culture. So began our dying.

My people are a wise people. I do not claim God accorded them special preference in the allocation of grey matter. That would be absurd; as absurd as the claims of superiority made by 'the ones without colour', the ones we came to call *umlungu*.[1]

But my people are patient. We have a saying: 'These mountains were here when we were born. They will be here long after we are gone.' Patiently, my people observed the world of which they knew they were a part – equal with the land, the rivers, the trees, the mountains and every other living thing.

My people knew how to flow with nature's rhythm, dance to its tune and harness its forces for their good. They knew about using and using up. They knew that rest is the beginning of restoration and that it brings healing.

How can one stand under the heavens one night, look up at the sky, point out one star and say: 'That star is mine!'? My people would have thought anyone mad who suddenly pronounced themselves sole owner of such and such a mountain, valley, river or any other piece of the earth.

They had not learnt the greed that brings fences with it. Later, when the newcomers cut up the land, cut it up until it bled, the stakes driven hard into its very heart, the barbed wire strangling it of breath, my people found themselves lessened, reduced. They were fenced in. They could no longer heal the land.

The strangers had come with new laws to the land they had 'discovered'. They imposed these laws on the people they found there and made sure they themselves were not bound by them. They were exclusively for my people. *Makhulu*[2] used to say to me: 'Grandchild of mine, a person has a definite nature, and if something is good you can be sure they will keep it for themselves.'

My people could no longer heal the land. They could not restore it when it was exhausted. The law forbade them to move pasture. A person's place of dwelling became their place of dying. We lost freedom of movement – the land lost the right to rest and restoration.

Fenced in. Forced to till exhausted land, we could not feed ourselves. But, you see, even that was no accident. The no-colour people had planned it all. They did nothing without planning it through and through – years in advance.

To feed his children, to feed his wife and his aged parents, a man was forced to go to the ones with eyes that have colour. And beg them to use his strength as they would use a horse. For that they would give him the shiny buttons without holes they had brought with them. This had become the only thing of value. It was hard to come by it. The scrubbed ones made sure they kept it under lock and key all the time. And never gave my people enough to get the things it was supposed to give them: food, clothing, medicine, anything. You could be dying, but without this button, *umlungu*, the ones without colour, would not give you medicine.

Umlungu's law said we could not dig for roots: it said we could not gather healing herbs. 'Miserly is the white man, indeed. He even withholds ochre, which he himself does not use – *Uyabandeza umlungu. Ude abandeze imbola engayiqabi!'* exclaimed my people, flabbergasted. For this kind of stinginess was new to them.

Ochre is the red powder with which we adorned ourselves. Now it was illegal to dig the ground for it. Resistance was strong, there were infringements galore. But by the time my own mother was a young woman ochre had already become a thing of the past.

Umlungu had an even better way of weaning us from our ways. Backward. Heathen. Things of the dark. Those are some of the labels he gave all things essentially us. The things that defined our uniqueness. In time, we learnt to hate them ourselves. To scorn those who adhered to them, who refused to 'go with the times', those we saw as hesitant 'to enter the world of electricity, the world of light'.

Instead of ochre and herbs, roots and other powders, we started using *umlungu's* creams. They promised us 'eternal youthfulness, glowing, wrinkle-free skin'. We didn't stop to think that our skin was already free of wrinkles, well into grand old age. We were being civilised. And happily did we stretch our necks for the yoke.

Umlungu's ways have an essential ingredient called Progress. Where Mama started with Metamorphosa, graduated to Karoo Freckle and Complexion

Cream and Bu-tone Cream for a Lovelier Complexion, now, in her nineties, she is on Oil of Olay, that bona fide fountain of youth. But Mama is far, far luckier than I am.

I am a true product of *umlungu*'s enlightenment. My face never was touched by such crudity as ochre or any of those things rural women – whom, basking in our new-found sophistication, we called backward – used on their faces. I started on Pond's Face Cream as a pre-teen. I was into Karoo Freckle and Complexion Cream by my adolescence. And in my early twenties, like millions of African women my age, I was breaking new ground. By this time, Progress had brought black people an elixir. Skin Lightening Creams.

And *umlungu* said he was doing what he was doing for our own good. He couldn't understand our gross stupidity. He had a duty to stop us from doing harm to ourselves. The yawning dongas[3] crisscrossing the land told *umlungu* it was the women digging for their cosmetics that were to blame; it was our large herds of cattle, the women gathering firewood. So said the dongas to *umlungu*.

But, to my people, the bleeding soil sang a different song; a song of mourning. And, in the manner of our tradition, my people passed the history on:

'These white people and their fences! They have killed the land.'

'They came with no cattle. But today we are the ones without cattle, while they boast ever-swelling herds.' 'Our land has been stolen. We live in fenced-in toy plots. Look at their farms! You can ride across them for a whole day without reaching the other side.'

With hearts more sorrow-filled with each dying day, my people watched their cattle getting thinner, their herds dwindle – and the youth of the nation die in rock falls in the mines of the colourless ones, who made them dig for gold they would never own.

'The land died with the coming of *umlungu*', said my people. And the mothers wailed: 'We lose our sons in mines of greed, mines our eyes have never seen, for gold we never touch.' Young women, their husbands away too long, swallowed by the mines, fretted: 'Do not forget me, my love, in the land of gold. Do not forget me, beloved. My heart, daily, yearns for you.' We became part-time parents to our children.

The fences of the colourless ones were not yet finished. There was more to come. *Umlungu* didn't care about the problems he made for my people. What did it matter that a mother, for lack of firewood, could not cook for her children? *Umlungu* had a bigger problem: deforestation.

We had no experience of hoarding, of planning for scarcity when there was enough. We had not learnt that one person might exact a price from another. We gave freely what God had already given.

Umlungu said he was not starving us. We could always buy firewood. Go to the shop and use the button without holes, he said. His brother who owned the shop wanted plenty of that button. But the button didn't like my people at all. It took one look, made a sharp U-turn and went right back whence it came. The coloured-eyed people hoarded it all. And the gold. And the land. To own. While we still wondered: how can a person claim a star as a personal possession?

Our fathers and our brothers, they toiled hard for that button without a hole. They suffered insults, broke their bodies and lost their lives. The button remained unmoved by our sacrifice. It was of one mind with those who had brought it. It would never change allegiance.

Poor as we were – my generation of women – we used a lot of buttons without holes buying the creams that bleached our skin. We listened to *umlungu*'s promises of a better life. If only we could rid ourselves of our colour, scour it off, like some dirty foreign matter. How we pursued the dream! At last we would be like them, the people who had brought us all these things of light. How we 'chased' the mirage: Ambi Skin Lightening Cream, Super Rose, Clear Tone, Astra ... and others too many to list here.

Like the fences on the land, the creams made *umlungu* plenty, plenty of buttons without holes ... and killed our skin. Just like the fences had killed the land. Today thousands of us walk around with ugly, dark blotches on our faces, a disfigurement. The land has the scarring dongas and we have these hideous marks.

We have no name for this disease in my language, or in any of the indigenous languages of the land. 'Chloasma' *umlungu* calls that which sits on our faces like fungus on a plant. Chloasma.[4] And he has a cure for it. If you can give him many, many buttons without a hole.

2.
CLAWING AT STONES

This essay was published in the 2001 collection edited by Mark Robert Waldman, The Spirit of Writing: Classic and Contemporary Essays Celebrating the Writing Life. *In it, Sindiwe Magona describes how she became a reader and later a writer and outlines the personal and political challenges she faced as a black South African writer when attempting to record the extreme circumstances of apartheid.*

Fear of Change

I have seen the thick welted scars
on people rudely plucked from hearth
And home. Bound hand and bleeding foot.
Kicked, punched, raped and ravaged
Every which way you dare to think.
Killed, in their millions and
Dumped on icy wave.

And today, those unlucky enough to
survive the gruesome plunder
annoy the world by failing to be quite,

quite human. By falling short of accepted
standards of civilisation. Never mind that
on these people, was performed a
National Lobotomy, that has left them with
No tongue of their own.[1]

I was in my thirties before I ever held a book written by a black woman in my hand; that was Maya Angelou's *I Know Why the Caged Bird Sings*. Now I am in my fifties and have read a few more such books, not as many as could be reasonably expected, given our numbers – in 2022, Africa alone has over 700 million women.[2] However, for reasons too many, too painful, sickeningly familiar and inseparable as resin from bark in our lives, the vast majority of African women and women of African descent have yet to tell their stories.

I am no historian. Thus, in my case the telling cannot be in that mode. History's dry exactitude kills the story: too many details simply disappear. My personal preference is music. If I could sing, I would have left songs that spoke of incredible beauty and unspeakable horror, for I have witnessed such things as make me want to shout about them from the mountaintops: the courage of women, forced to live whole lifetimes without their husbands. In my poetry, I call these women 'gold widows', as their men slaved hard in the gold mines of Johannesburg for gold that they and their women would never see, never wear. Meanwhile, alone in the damned villages, the women kept home, family and communities intact. They raised children, sowed and reaped fields, nursed the sick, and buried the dead – women dug graves and put corpses to rest. When, in desperation, they went to work in towns, domestic servants to white women, they became the invisible, recyclable hands that made things work, getting little for their pains.

I was there in 1950 when women marched, protesting the Pass Laws. They went to the Pass Office in Langa and, in an act of desperate courage, burned their pass books: the police, the white superintendent and his cronies watching, the women burned their passes.

I have also seen the most vile acts of man. Evil. Chief Albert Luthuli[3] and Steve Biko[4] are heroes who were killed because of their opposition to apartheid. Many others remain nameless skeletons hikers have since stumbled across on isolated mountains, or their corpses became manure on obscure Boer farms. We, the Africans against whom that evil was fully unleashed, have survived apartheid. But in fact the whole country has survived apartheid. The whole country. For none were (or could have been) left untainted by such evil. Yet the full story of apartheid has still to be told, and I want to be part of that telling. If only I could sing! Thousands would cram into the world's most famous music halls and sacred stadiums, come to hear me sing of sorrow … and of joy.

Of humiliation … and of triumph. Of terrible loss … and of our redemption.

Alas, I cannot sing. But I have always enjoyed stories. Those told to me around the fire in the village of my birth, Gungululu, by my grandmothers. And, later, those that came to me via the written page.

As a child, I loved reading. Whenever I could lay my hands on a book, even the play I enjoyed, perhaps to excess, suffered. Books were prized possessions – I suppose precisely because of their scarcity. I come from peasant stock, and no one ever read me to sleep as a child. The only books my parents ever bought were those demanded by the school. Like most Africans of their generation in South Africa, they'd had the most rudimentary of educations. Besides, we were dirt poor. Books and book buying had no business in our life. However, I was very fortunate that Jola, a neighbour, worked as a domestic servant in a white home. There must have been children about my age in that white family I will never know. Often, she brought back books and comics from her 'kitchen', as these places of employment are called by the women who slave their lives away in them. Thus, I grew up reading good British comics as well as classic children's books and it was with exceeding impatience that I waited for 'Jola's white people' to be throwing out books.

Those books and the stories they brought me – that was magic and mystery all rolled into one. The stories were, at one and the same time, about strange faces, strange places and even stranger happenings, that's true. But they were also about me. They gave me hope. This could also happen to me. I, also, could do this. When I'd finished reading the last book of a batch, I fell into a gloom. When would the next crop come? What stories would those books bring me? Where would those stories take place? Who would be doing what in them? The waiting was sheer torture. Therefore, mindful of the terrible inevitability of book endings and the long dry periods that threatened, when I might have absolutely nothing to read, I would read a book, especially the last of a batch, with artful slowness: stopping when I sensed that something exciting was about to happen, in eager anticipation; rereading whole chunks before proceeding after a pause.

And long before I came across enterprising teachers, I revelled in new words. When I met a new word for the first time, I immediately recognised it as a newcomer, a stranger whose acquaintance I had to make, an addition to my gem collection. With no dictionary to aid me (who had dictionaries in the African township then? who has them now?), I would attempt to decipher its meaning by examining its role, its function in the sentence, and, of course, within the realm of the story as a whole. Thereafter, I would try to use the new word myself. And do so as soon as opportunity presented itself. In class, I always came up with these clever expressions, phrases, or words no one else knew – to the delight of the teacher and the chagrin of my classmates, and my utter stupefaction that the other children failed to admire, applaud or feel the excitement I myself felt. I dare say mistakes were made in this manner of vocabulary building – but hey, I enjoyed the stories and marvelled as I whizzed through time and vast distances, well beyond the confines of Blouvlei, the sprawling tin-shack location where I was growing up, to places of splendour and grandeur, of the mystical and the magical, of excitement and adventure.

However, even then I recognised that, important as the story's details and actions were, the more significant aspect, the power and magic, lay in the telling. Knowing nothing of story technique, I nevertheless fully understood there was a difference in *how* stories were told – thanks to those village evening sessions of my childhood where, around a fire, we children often heard the same story from different tellers. I grew up, therefore, aware that the same story sounded much more interesting (or less so), depending on who was telling it or, indeed, what mood, emphasis or nuance the same teller brought to its telling. It is from these fireside storytellers' sessions that I learnt that the audience has to be engaged from the very start of the tale. *Iintsomi*, the Xhosa folktales of my early childhood, are begun with a short call and response format:

'*Kwathi ke kaloku ngantsomi!*'[5] is what the teller opens with.

'*Chosi!*'[6] respond the listeners. And throughout, the audience is actively involved, clapping or singing or chanting responses. Today, I read, and I enjoy the convenience that comes with this method of story sharing. But the thrill of the oral story is well-remembered – it still rushes through me.

The creative process has always been sacred to me, and although I grew up with no role models in the practice, I've always enjoyed writing. As a pupil, if the teacher was going to read an essay to the class, invariably, that essay would be mine. And I was not averse to the flattery such recognition implied. Later, as an elementary teacher, I found it very hard to grade essays. Grammar and spelling errors would go unmarked (and unpunished) while I marvelled at the creative genius of a young artist. The unknown worlds reading opens up to me are an endless source of awe and inspiration.

As late as 1990, I stumbled on the sad statistic that in South Africa, since African women had first began writing and publishing (in any genre, any language), only five women had accomplished that feat. Five! I write to change that – to bear witness, to tell those who will people this world long after I have gone what it was I saw, heard, experienced. They need to know who we were and what we were about. I believe future readers will appreciate hearing our perspective of things. Forced removals and the brutal scattering of the African community in South Africa killed the oral tradition, through which the history of the nation was preserved. However, the imperative of preservation not only stands but, doubtless, is even more urgent today, more urgent than ever before. Therefore, I write to leave footsteps.

Writing brings me healing. It is therapeutic. Writers generally write about what they know. And that knowledge is sometimes far from pleasant. But it is in writing about our disappointments, our failures, our losses, our defeats, our pain and suffering, that we discover the startling fact that we have survived all this and perhaps even thrived – despite the challenges such setbacks may have forced us to face.

Also, I am learning that writing is a long journey. Even in these times of modern travel, a journey can be full of surprises, unpredictable, and fraught with danger. Delays, handicaps, deceptive companions, and tantalising distractions abound. One's mettle is sorely tested in this process.

The present lap of my journey began when writing my late father's (still unpublished) biography. The first surprise was that the outpouring came in the form of poetry. I offered no resistance, but revelled in this new and unfamiliar form. Some sixty pages into the story, Father's family welcomes his bride. I anticipated as many (if not more) pages as I began writing about his life as experienced by us, his children. Naturally, this would include Mama. Then there'd be a book of poetry in two parts! But Mama survived Tata by almost thirty years. Should she not get a part of her own? Voila: Penrose and Lilian, a biography of my parents, in verse, in three parts!

From this, it can be correctly surmised that I was having a wonderful time driving down memory lane, remembering and recapturing the essence of my parents, as it seemed to me, at least. However, traveller beware: there may be mines on the road you're taking.

Father worked in the gold mines of Johannesburg before I was born. I was in my thirties when I first laid eyes on Magubane's *South Africa*, with its photos of 'mine boys'. That book angered and disgusted me. But it wasn't till I came to the corresponding part of my father's life that a mule kicked me full in the belly. All this time, more than two decades afterwards, the despicable things those photos depicted still shocked me. Grown men 'naked as unpodded beans ... dusted with sprayings of DDT', as I wrote in my poem 'Mine Boys',[7] forced to show their anuses, the regular inspection against theft of precious stones – the vicious truth had never before penetrated my defences.

Father worked in the mines. Mine bosses did such things to mine 'boys'. But that such things were done to Father never occurred to me. How do you look at the man you have known all your life as 'Protector, Provider, Soother of spirits bruised'[8] and admit to yourself he suffered unimaginable violation, endured unspeakable humiliation? How does a child love and respect a father and know that that man has been treated in a manner no animal ever suffered, and knowing that there are many who saw him as less than human? How do you swallow a father's bitter impotence?

I wept when the realisation hit me. When I could no longer deny that my father underwent such brutality, a sorrow so intense overcame me. And, I wept for my father. For all the men who have to leave their wives and their children, every year, for eleven months of the year, to go to a place of shadows, of unfulfilled dreams, of promises false. Where lives are slighted, wasted, ill-used and squandered; sacrificed to greed and need, real and manufactured. Where rich men dream of richer reaches; And poor men die clawing at stones.

Do I wish I had not begun the project? Has the pain the revelation brought made me wish to write less or stay away from intimate subjects?

No! To the contrary. I now recognise that this pain is an integral part of who I am. The need to mine the past, even as I witness the present, is an honour I accept without question. For all the vexing perplexity this might bring, I am convinced that it is only by probing both the joys and woundings of time that we might be blessed and empowered to influence the future.

3.
FINDING MY WAY HOME

In this essay, which expands upon a piece with the same title that was first published in the popular South African magazine Fairlady *in June 2003, Sindiwe Magona reflects upon her reasons for returning to South Africa after a 22-year stay in the United States, and describes her efforts to help rebuild the country through her writing.*

ONE DAY I will write an essay, 'All My Mothers', because I have been blessed with an array of human beings who have been very loving towards me: my parents; my grandparents; my aunts and (most of) my uncles; the extended family; and my teacher in Standard 2, dear Miss Vuyelwa Mabija (*A Ndlovu!*[1]). This list includes a number of men because by 'mothers' I mean all those who made me who I am today, whether female or male, old or young.

After lunch break one day, Miss Mabija took us out of the classroom onto a little hill. It was the first lesson I'd had on writing. She brought an orange. She made us look at it, and she made us feel it, our eyes closed. She made us look at it with our eyes open, then smell it and taste it. There must have been thirty or forty of us, but we all ended up with little pieces of the peel, the rind, the fruit, the succulence, the little things in the orange that burst open inside you. Today, whenever I write, I think of that lesson, how this woman taught us to describe and write about an orange. The ease with which she went about it was nothing short of magical, for not only did she manage to get us into the orange, inside and out, she empowered us, gave us an invisible magic wand. That day I, for one, was gifted with belief in my ability to say, describe, tell anyone anything, anywhere, any time. *Ndlovu zidl' ekhaya ngokuswel' umalusi!*[2]

When I became a young woman, my family marked the occasion with a ceremony we call *intonjane*. This announces to the community that the girl has now become a young woman. It also involves an initiation process which is similar to a boy's circumcision ritual in that, while it does not involve an incision of any kind, it does require that the girl be secluded for some weeks and trained in the ways of adulthood by the women in her extended family. It is a shame we have, in our haste to be civilised and westernised and Christianised, let go of so many of our rituals, because they remain significant.

Just before my retirement, I went to the bar mitzvah of a friend's son. During the course of the proceedings, which left me in absolute awe, I found myself thinking, 'How can this child, this boy of 13, ever forget where he belongs?' The sense of belonging at that celebration was palpable. That you are connected to the whole community when the village stops to honour a young person, and for that one day he or she is the centre of the universe – how can you ever forget that? You have been honoured, and you cannot disgrace the family, the community or the group of people to whom you belong and who hold you in such esteem. Sometimes when things don't go right for you, it helps to remember who you are and where you come from. If nobody ever told you, or made you realise that you are a loved human being, a worthy human being, highly valued, what have you got to lose?

My family, even with their limited means, had given me a good start in life. I ended up with something called the Higher Primary Teacher's Certificate. In my first year of teaching, at the age of 19, I got pregnant. The Department of Bantu Education put me on a two-year suspension, but before the period was up, I was pregnant again. It was 1965, and I decided to get married, but this put me in the subclass of teachers who could only be hired on a one-year temporary basis, though only if no unmarried women or male candidates were available. Marriage had made a terrible situation worse. I explored other avenues, including working in a restaurant, but each time apartheid blocked me: according to the law, a prospective Bantu employee had to have clearance from Coloured Affairs before being hired. So I decided that it was easier, in the long run, to take a job as a domestic worker. And then, when I was expecting child number three, my husband upped and left.

Nothing in my upbringing had prepared me for single parenthood or for this abandonment. Imagine my shock when it happened – I was four months pregnant. Because I was not divorced, I wasn't considered a breadwinner by the department, never mind that I had three children, so I was not allowed to teach. Of course, I was not a citizen in my own country either, so I could not apply for welfare. I was so angry with my husband for abandoning us and with the government for being an active and forceful obstacle. I was damn angry as a young woman; I just felt it was so unfair. But I never forgot I belonged; that my birth family and clan, relatives, neighbours and congregants from the Church thought I was a person of worth. These people expected me to live up to my responsibilities. My children, fatherless now, had become my sole responsibility. I was filled with anger, frustration and shame. In this state of mind, I came up with a slogan, which surprises me now, looking at my wiser, younger self in my twenties. Anger, frustration, and shame being my daily dose, I coined a slogan. I used it to rev myself up and to kick start myself into action: '*Despite* the government, *in spite of* the government, *to spite* the government, *I will be something*!'

And, yes, I became something much better than even I could have dreamt of way back then. Now that I am finally grown up, a fact I can no longer deny as I face retirement, I appreciate even more what that slogan meant – the deeper meaning that was not quite clear to me then. Ah! The power of agency. You are the only person who can direct your life. Yes, others may, and, more often than not, do help – but you have to be, must be, the prime director. If you can't or won't or are unwilling, reluctant or doubtful, no amount of help will achieve the desired outcomes; you will remain where you are, if you're lucky, you'll remain where you are and stagnate. Or worse, you might sink even lower into the bottomless pit that is poverty.

We have all seen or heard of instances of brilliant students with heaps of financial resources at their disposal and an array of education institutions that they could attend, who finally end up not completing the studies they'd embarked upon. My great fortune, and achieving so much from such a humbling start, is not lost on me.

Then, on the verge of retirement, came the miracle of South Africa's transformation – a new democracy – and, for me, the birth of a brand new dream. With this change, I started dreaming of being part of the transformation in my birth country. At that time/moment, I had the opportunity to retire in the United States, having served the United Nations for more than fifteen years. Instead, I chose to take the 'Repatriation' package rather than applying for a Green Card, even though many of my friends urged me to stay. But South Africa was the country of my origin and a part of the world that was most dear to my heart. I knew that I needed to write about what moved or bothered me and to focus on issues about which I had very strong feelings. It just made more sense, everything considered, to return. For while I love all humanity and I love the world in its entirety, there can be no denying my partiality towards the land of my birth, with all its flaws, failures and missteps – then and now – for I love this beautiful country and its beautiful people. I also chose to return because I had always felt that those of us Africans living in the diaspora and in exile, needed to return home to contribute to the development of Africa. A country is in trouble if it starts exporting its thinkers, creatives, intellectuals. The answer to the 1994 moment, as I saw it, was for South Africans to roll up our sleeves and work vigorously for social transformation. It would not just be a challenge, but an honour and a privilege to be part of the remaking of the nation.

It was in response to that singular privilege that I chose to return to my birth country. I made that decision as I truly believed that South Africans were blessed with an opportunity to create something new in a fledgling democracy. Not many people have that kind of opportunity in their own countries. Even as I geared myself for repatriation, I was painfully aware of the mammoth problems the country faced. Even then, I was aware of the heady excitement of the new political system that had replaced the system of apartheid which was now loathed by all, even by those whom it had abundantly benefitted, and who had adamantly supported it by returning the apartheid government with ever-increasing majorities during the whites-only elections. Still, it would not be an easy row to sow. Only a fool would think otherwise.

Understandably, those who were oppressed by the policies of apartheid hated it the most, and hate it still. Among the innumerable abominations apartheid visited on people not classified white, was poverty. Poverty that resulted from legislated barring of all black people from participating meaningfully in the economy of their country. It was common knowledge that poverty in South Africa was race related and that this would be one of the major challenges for the new government. What I feared personally was the disappointment awaiting many black people, most of whom believed their lives were about to improve and improve immediately, now that apartheid was over.

I knew differently. I knew, and that is why I write. Writing is my way of sharing. The second volume of my autobiography – *Forced to Grow* (1992) – describes how I escaped poverty. Getting the right to vote does not end anyone's poverty. I had seen clear evidence of this in countries in Africa that had achieved freedom from colonial rule only to fall into disarray. I am not apportioning blame. I am not saying they or their governments were at fault. But that that was the situation – and it still is – no one can deny.

So, I came home to use my pen to help South Africans confront the problems of the nation. As though poverty were not enough of a problem for the country to contend with, the HIV and Aids pandemic had also hit the world. It would be the poor, who were already dealing with the strife of poverty, that were most affected by the disease. Never getting a chance at wealth, it was all the more tragic that they were first in line for death.

Working in the Department of Public Information of the United Nations, I could never escape the news about my home country. And it was not good news. Even as everyone rejoiced, thrilled that the anti-apartheid battle had been won, the HIV and Aids crisis posed unprecedented danger. Poverty in South Africa, black poverty, that is, was old news. The international community could be counted on to do something about the alleviation of the plight of the poor in South Africa. Why? They had already been doing a lot during apartheid. Why would the world stop now when their efforts would not be hindered by the apartheid regime? They would be working with the full cooperation and appreciation of the new government. And remember who headed that government … heads of states were falling over one another to meet Rolihlahla Nelson Mandela, and everyone soon knew that the best way to get a meeting arranged was through 'donations', especially towards work on children. But all that goodwill and all those efforts were clouded by the new and devastating news of a deadly virus that could kill thousands upon thousands of men, women and children.

Even before I was back on home turf, I'd come to a fuller understanding of the gravity of the situation. I became an Aids activist through my writing, even while I was still working at the UN. Poetry flew fast and furious out of my pen, resulting in the only book of poetry to my name – *Please, Take Photographs!* (2009). I read one of these poems, 'Our House is on Fire', at a gathering on HIV and Aids at the UN. The poems, in turn, led to talks and more talks and more talks. Things really took off then, and my writing flowed: I was writing songs about Aids, and plays, including *Vukani!/Wake Up!* (2009). This play was aimed mainly at destroying the stupid myth that 'sleeping with a virgin cures Aids'.

But these efforts seemed not to be enough. 'Not enough!' the raging virus screamed at me, 'Not enough!' Nothing I did, nothing any of us did in this country or, indeed, the world, seemed to be enough. In South Africa, aggravating factors were numerous. For starters, our government was busy undermining the best efforts of Aids activists who were interrogated and pilloried, with attempts to nullify their courageous efforts. What the whole world admitted, our government denied.

Eventually, five whole years later, the untenable situation would provoke a post-retirement novel, *Beauty's Gift* (2008). The book garnered praise from leading Aids activists in the country and this gave me hope that we were headed in the right direction.

Beauty's Gift was reissued in 2018 and graciously welcomed by publisher, writer, poet and activist Karina Magdalena Szczurek with the following comments in her review of the novel:

> *Beauty's Gift* offers a space for identification and understanding for women which is an enormous gift in itself. It is a difficult book to read, because it reveals truths about our society and the people closest to us which are hard to accept. But exposing and confronting them is the first step to a better future for all.[3]

If the novel does indeed accurately capture the experience of living at this moment of unimaginable crisis and expose the deeper truths regarding HIV and Aids, I am reminded of my gratitude to Miss Mabija and what she taught me about the powers of observation through her exercise of describing an orange. Keen observations and brutal truths are what we need now – perhaps more so than any other time in recent history.

4.

IT IS IN THE BLOOD: TRAUMA AND MEMORY IN THE SOUTH AFRICAN NOVEL

This essay, which was featured in the 2012 collection Trauma, Memory, and Narrative in the Contemporary South African Novel, *strives to explain the preoccupation with trauma in the South African novel. Sindiwe Magona highlights the pervasive and extreme nature of the oppression enacted upon South Africans under apartheid and argues that the effects of the resultant traumas are still experienced in tangible and damaging ways.*

TRAUMA MAY BE described as a morbid condition produced by wounds or external violence. Psychological trauma is not visible the way bodily trauma is – it is what we call emotional shock. The dictionary tells us it is 'a violent emotional blow, especially one which has a lasting psychic effect; a neurological condition from physical or emotional injury'.[1] Note that we're not talking of just any kind of shock, but of an emotional shock that creates substantial and lasting damage to the psychological development of the individual (generally leading to neurosis). Moreover, such shock must be produced by violence. Also, it results in debilitation, and the traumatised person exhibits diminished functioning or functioning is wholly destroyed.

We see, then, that 1) there must be violence, and 2) that the violence must be such that it so traumatises the individual that the result is destruction of normal functioning to varying degrees – from mild, to severe, to total collapse.

If, then, this is the definition of trauma – a morbid condition produced by violence – little wonder that the South African novel is preoccupied with trauma. As my title indicates, trauma is *in the blood* for the people of South Africa; they can neither escape it nor ignore it. To do the latter would be well-nigh impossible except perhaps in those individuals who have escaped into madness; and the former is just not possible, as trauma itself, its residue, or its outcomes, form an integral, inescapable part of their very lives, of life itself – of all life in South Africa. Psychological trauma is one of the legacies of apartheid and has resulted in the social neurosis daily witnessed in the country – as evidenced by the screaming headlines: appalling violence and acts of unimaginable savagery.

My people, amaXhosa, say *'Isegazini'*[2] when something shows itself to be such an integral part of someone's makeup that the two – the individual and the act/compulsion towards that act – display an inescapable dance of fatality; when the person shows an inherent inability to divorce himself/herself from a habit that is clearly not wholesome and may even be harmful either to self and/or to others. However, even though clearly aware and understanding the consequences of that particular action or course of action – despite all that – the individual consistently engages in this destructive behaviour. In other words, the destructive behaviour appears wholly and totally ineluctable – inevitable.

It is in the blood. It is generally accepted and understood that blood is essential to human life; without blood there can be no living. Sayings such as 'He bled to death' show the truthfulness of that. How, then, does a person so embrace a habit that it becomes or shows itself to be an integral part of that life – something without which the person simply could not live, showing no inclination or capability to live free of it?

Fact: South Africa has had a violent past.

Fact: South Africa has a violent present.

Fact: South Africa will predictably have a violent future – unless …

This is not a prophecy – it is a prediction based on present trends or the sad state of the nation, as far as safety is concerned. We talk of the 'legacy of apartheid'. Invariably, when you hear the phrase, you can bet your bottom dollar that what the speaker is referring to is negative in the extreme. That is because apartheid, a nefarious, evil system, could not but bear highly poisonous fruit.

What, you may be asking yourself by now, has all this got to do with writing? What has it got to do with the novel? Writers write out of compulsion. They are compelled to write. The grist for the mill is the world they inhabit, and each writer defines that world in a peculiarly individual manner. So, each will tell the story according to ability, inclination, 'mood of the moment' or the level of provocation of an incident. However, all writers live under the same sky, breathe in the same air, and generally watch the same television, read or listen to the same news; therefore, there are bound to be some similarities or overlaps in, certainly, the subject or issues with which they are concerned and about which they write. As might be expected, the novel in South Africa, even after the end of apartheid, is more apt to deal with trauma. This is, indeed, not at all surprising. Apartheid South Africa was a traumatic place in which to live, the times and the manner of living inescapably scarring.

I look at my own writing and am alarmed. I ask myself: What is the point of my writing? Am I hooked on trauma and the traumatic? Can I write about nothing save that which is wounding? My last published book – a volume of poetry entitled *Please, Take Photographs* – strikes me as an example of such. Consider the title poem, the pain of it, urging parents to 'take photographs' of their children, so that on days of remembrance they may look at those, the children long gone.[3] These are young people destined, so the medical scientists tell us, not to live to see their thirtieth birthday. The horror! I am reminded of why I felt compelled to put into words the pain of a nation slowly dying from a plague that comes through love and loving – the most intimate form of human interaction.

Trauma assumes that an ordinary life is disturbed in a manner so violent that the harm will last. Therefore, we assume a healthy beginning into which comes rude and violent wounding, resulting in trauma. In South Africa, perhaps the single most violent event in the nation's history was the coming of the white tribes to the continent. That resulted in the struggle for resources, mainly land, with the eventual subjugation of the African and consequent clash of cultures – a clash which ended in the complete domination of the indigenous culture by the invading culture. The ensuing trauma turned endemic. Its effects will be felt for generations to come.

I ask myself: Will my writing *always* be about the traumatic aspects of life in South Africa? I then answer myself, tell myself that life under apartheid was no ordinary experience. It is trauma when a man is never allowed to live with his lawfully wedded wife all the days of his working life; never sees his children grow; is never allowed to enjoy family life until he is too old or too ill to work – when he is then ejected back into the rural area in which he has not lived as an adult. Hoodwinked into marriage by the church that cries it is 'sin' to bed a woman without the benefit of marriage, only to be condemned to perpetual bachelorhood by the migrant labour system. A beast of burden. When did he ever get a chance to model to his son what a man is? What a man does? What a man does not do? And today, we wonder that African men seem to have forgotten the meaning of fatherhood. Recent survey results, published by the Institute of Race Relations, show that an alarming 70 per cent of African children live as paternal orphans![4] But then, when and how could African boys and young men learn what it means to be a father when they themselves grew up with fathers perpetually absent, off in far-away cities or farms or mines?

Is it not trauma when one is born into inescapable, grinding poverty, where the working poor remain stubbornly, desperately poor despite their daily toil under the most unfavourable conditions? But these men and women toil for wages guaranteed never to uplift them from squalor; the employers perceive them as barely human. Is this not trauma, never to know for sure where the next meal is coming from; never to have all the things you need at school while the government allows you the dubious freedom of not going to school? Is it not trauma, when you are at the bottom of the dunghill as the government divides up the spoils for the education of the country's children thus: white child: R480; coloured child: R280; black child: R28? This, as late as the mid-1980s. Of course, African children were the only ones who did not 'suffer' under compulsory education; by law, white, coloured, and Indian children had to stay at school until the age of 16. The apartheid government was at least honest enough to admit it could not force children whose education it did not fund to go to school!

Africans did not enjoy property rights or the right to own 'immovable property' – which, in plain English, means a house or land. Imagine that: going through life slaving but never free from poverty, and then, as though that were not insult enough, enough injury, enough trauma – to be legally forbidden to own a home of one's own! Never to mother one's children – working 'sleep-in' at a white family's home, minding that family's white children, day and night, while the parents work, study, or party/entertain. It is clear, therefore, that for Africans, marriage was really a myth. They went through the motions of getting married, legalising the union, but never enjoyed what is usually taken for granted by husbands and wives – common domicile.

Africans, in South Africa, did not enjoy citizenship. Never a citizen in the country of one's birth, as white South Africa pursued the myth of a country in which there were no black citizens, by the simple expedient of dispossessing them of what is internationally considered a person's birthright. Can you imagine worse wounding? And this is just the tip of the iceberg. We could be here till kingdom come if I were inclined or had the time to go through the whole catastrophe of the implications of living under apartheid – the daily fancy footwork necessary to remain in urban areas when the illusive 'permission' disappeared. No doubt, the South African nation will bear the brunt of this designed ineptitude for decades to come. We saw the gruesome necklacings of the 1980s and 1990s; we are plagued with the rape of children and infants; inter-generational sex is fast becoming 'acceptable'; part-time fatherhood, whereby a man has numerous children by sundry women, no longer raises an eyebrow. Talk about diminished functioning!

One could ask: are those not symptoms of a neurosis? In other words, is our normalcy really normal or is it aberration? However, let us focus our minds on trauma and narrative in the contemporary South African novel. As stated before, the novelist, the storyteller, draws from life. This, therefore, implies the employment of memory. It is not surprising, then, that today, in South Africa, the novelist still draws on life as it was lived in that country in the not-too-distant past. Memory of lived experience informs her; it informs her work. Memory of what she has witnessed, directly or indirectly. But what is memory? When does memory begin and where is it lodged?

We've heard or read of people who recall events from early childhood. That is memory. However, there is another kind of memory. Psychologists seem to suggest that there is a significant difference between the physical architecture of the developing brain of children who are socially stimulated and that of children who are deprived of such stimulation in the first three years of life. Furthermore, psychologists assert that this has huge implications for later development and behaviour. For whether, in their teens, these deprived children will be fully socialised to become hoodlums. It is in the blood! Our bodies are perforated by painful memory – trauma – which is in the blood, in the very cells of our gnarled, apartheid-deformed bodies; which is why, when something triggers a certain memory from the hideous and painful past, often the response is visceral, the outward, demonstrable behaviour immediate and astounding to those who lack comprehension of who we are, and the dehumanisation we've suffered. Our bodies embody the pain of our legalised enslavement.

In light of all this, what can I write about? What do I remember? What is in my memory? 'Write about what you know!' we are often told. We all heard Mandla Langa's chilling account of what he has been doing with and through his writing:[5] remembering and exorcising a painful memory. Memory and trauma. It is precisely this awareness of me, of my memory, the memory of my race, that made me bold enough to come out as a poet late in 1993. Yes, like everybody else (with a few exceptions, of course) I was exceedingly happy, exhilarated, to see apartheid go. However, perhaps unlike many, my happiness was tempered with a large dollop of reality. It was not for naught that apartheid was labelled 'a crime against humanity'. An understanding, often stated, was that apartheid was dehumanising. In other words, dehumanised, we, South Africans, came to our freedom. Bleeding, broken, we came to freedom. Who, then, told us we would be (automatically) re-humanised? Who waved what magic wand to get us what we had lost, what we had been robbed of? What made us think that just because we could vote this meant we were well, whole, and mended?

Taking all the above into account, I not only wrote 'Fear of Change', a poem about the imminent advent of uhuru, but actually read the poem publicly – in New York, where I lived at the time. A first for me!

I wrote this poem because I know that systems perpetuate themselves. What made us think that, just because every four or five years we can now *all* vote, we were mended, cured, and rehabilitated? To this day, if you take a four-year-old from a family where the grandparents and parents were doctors, and you ask that toddler to bring you a stethoscope from a whole array of objects on a table … guess what? That baby will go and pick out the designated object! I was in my thirties before I knew what that thing that dangled from the doctor's neck was called! On an education diet at the bottom of the R480:280:28 scale, what child growing up in the squatter camps of this country would be able to name a stethoscope before – if they were exceedingly lucky – they went to college? That is systemic violence, the resultant pain and suffering not only inescapable – it is in the blood. The forced removals of the 1950s are still etched in our memories. The resulting dislocation lost us the graves of our loved ones. The distance was just too huge to negotiate – physically, financially, and, above all, emotionally. We bled. We are still bleeding. The memory of that collective wound festers still.

Accepting that apartheid, by its illiberal nature, was against or worked against the ordinary, natural development and growth of a person from birth to maturation, we must then agree that it warped that individual, made her/him something different from what they might have become. It was agreed internationally that apartheid dehumanised – not only warped, but actively damaged – the human being, spiritually and physically. Look at the obvious physical bonsais it made of the poorest of the poor! We all know that height is a function of diet while the child is growing. Look at the Springbok rugby players – it is not a challenge to see who never lacked proper nutrition as a child.

Not so long ago, the children in the village benefitted immensely from traditional *iintsomi*[6] told around the fire of an evening. These tales treated life as it was lived and were an integral part of the socialisation of the African child. Alas, the villages of South Africa are well-nigh ghost villages, thanks to urbanisation. This has resulted in the displacement of the grandparents, the traditional storytellers. Have we thrown away the baby with the bath water?

Those folktales and the life I have lived and witnessed around me are embedded in my memory. What can I write about, therefore? What can I write about except the memory of the race? By race, I do not mean an ethnic group but those with whom I share similar experiences, and these people vary in accordance with those experiences: women, when referring to how the world treats (or mistreats) me as a member of that group; black people or people of colour, when that is applicable; the working class; single parents; the poor and the excluded, the denigrated, the despised. The contemporary South African novelist has had a large dollop of reality served up on her plate.

In André Brink's *A Dry White Season*, first published in 1979, we see apartheid at work, at its most obdurate. The protagonist is a white man by the name of Ben du Toit. He is a teacher and at his school there is a labourer, Gordon Ngubeni. We witness a relationship between the two – not friendship, but the kind that used to exist and still exists between master and servant, when a step beyond the ordinary is taken … as sometimes happens. The teacher becomes interested in the life of the handyman. This is already unusual, for, during apartheid, the only relationship between most white people and black people was of the master-servant kind and very few white people allowed themselves to step out of the prescribed and accepted 'traditional way of life'.

The handyman, Ngubeni, has a son who is in school. Du Toit pays his school fees; for that kindness, the boy, Jonathan, tends the garden for Du Toit over weekends. Trouble starts when the boy takes part in politics and is killed by the police – not that the police admit this, of course. But no one in the township believes the story of Jonathan's death as told by the police. His father certainly doesn't; however, because Ngubeni is known to him, Du Toit takes an unusual interest in the case. What is more, he puts his money where his mouth is and pays for the lawyers. However, soon Ngubeni, too, is killed by the police. The trouble does not stop there but spreads, engulfing and destroying not only the Ngubeni family – son, father, and finally mother – but that of the family's benefactor, the teacher. Du Toit's family cracks and eventually breaks up as a result of his stepping out of line, crossing the colour line, so to speak, not minding his own business but getting himself involved in the affairs of 'the Other'. Once Du Toit embarks on that 'not traditional' trip, he is soon driven beyond, way beyond, what he'd ever contemplated. We see him go to the black township, legally out of bounds for the likes of him. Predictably, he lands in very hot water, not from his pursuers, the police, but from those he would help. This is a moment of rude awakening for the benefactor of black people.

He then paints a vivid picture of the violence that ensues as he enters the township. Set upon by an angry crowd, he is kicked and punched, but manages to fight his attackers off and find his way back into the car. As someone tries to grab his leg he desperately pleads, 'Don't you understand? I'm on your side!'[7] By way of reply, a stone is hurled as the crowd closes in on him. Panicked, he reverses the car, sending the attackers flying, before he sets off. But he encounters more angry people determined to prevent his escape. They too are armed, and more stones and bricks rain down on the car, one breaking the window, narrowly missing him. For a split second he loses control, and is surprised and grateful that in his blind, desperate getaway, children and animals all over the place, none are hurt. Later, in attempting to justify his actions – 'I wanted to help. Right.'[8] – he glimpses the inescapable racial divide that is life in South Africa. Irrespective of how sincerely he might sympathise with black people, this did nothing to breach the gulf between his good intentions and their outcomes. He cannot actually be in the shoes of the oppressed; imagination can never become reality. It is in that moment of clarity that he sees how entrenched race hate and division are in the country he loves. Nothing he or anyone can do will change that: 'I remain white, and favoured by the very circumstances I abhor. Even if I'm hated, and ostracised, and persecuted, and in the end destroyed, nothing can make me black.'[9]

Eventually, with all the main characters gone, only Du Toit – by now estranged from his wife and two daughters and their husbands (only his son still speaks to him) – is left as target. And pursue him the police do not fail to do. Until his death, when he is run over by a car ... a hit-and-run.

In my epistolary novel, *Mother to Mother*, first published in 1998, a distraught mother confronts the heinous deed of her son – the apparently senseless murder of a young woman whose only 'crime' was the colour of her skin. The mother's grief drives her to cast her mind's eye back, recalling the history of that son's life. And what she dredges from her memory makes her say, 'It's been a long, hard road my son has travelled'.[10] She retraces some of the steps along that road, from his traumatic conception to his early childhood, abandonment by his father, his witnessing of police brutality – at a very tender age, and his possible implication in that gruesome act – grinding poverty, starting school –

with no possibility of ever possessing a full uniform – never enough to eat, never mind any consideration of nutrition, living in unending squalor, with no stimulation, his political awakening and the redirection of that to criminality, all legal avenues of participation in political life closed, barred – when the murderer's mother recalls that young man's life she gradually comes to see the intention behind her son's evil act for what it represents: 'the unconscious collective wish of the nation, [to] rid ourselves of the scourge'. She goes on to describe the murder as 'the eruption of a slow, simmering, seething rage', itself the result of 'the resentment of three hundred years' – 'that the oppressed harbour, have harboured, from generation to generation – carrying the scars, telling and listening [to] the stories of their suffering'.[11]

What is that, if not memory at work? A mother's memory of the hard and bitter life she has had, that her child has had. However, she also sees that life as representative – it is not just hers but that of her race, the race of the oppressed and dispossessed who have 'burning hatred for the oppressor', and they include 'My son, the blind but sharpened arrow of the wrath of his race. Your daughter, the sacrifice of hers.'[12]

We cannot but see that the cards were stacked against the son. Just as the cards were stacked against the Ngubeni family in Brink's *A Dry White Season*. Every system perpetuates itself.

In *Mother to Mother*, this all-embracing, long-suffering mother's vision speaks of the almost inevitable narrative rooted in memory – a narrative of pain and suffering, of trauma which will be revisited, time and time again. Certainly, in the South African novel; certainly, in the present and foreseeable future.

As can be seen in both novels, remembering plays a big part. Memory, the faculty or ability to recall, informs the individual. And this is not just individual memory but collective memory – the memory of the race. By race, remember, I do not mean a group that identifies itself as such by colour, geographical location, religion, gender or, indeed, a host of other determinants and definitions – the moneyed class, for instance. People do not only identify themselves as belonging to a particular group, but also hold certain beliefs precisely because of that; beliefs perpetuated, from generation to generation, through narrative – oral or written. Which is why, in South Africa (as elsewhere in the world), the trauma that the land has suffered is not only related to the trauma it continues to suffer, it has birthed it; for it is in the blood. The children of South Africa grew up with certain folklore. And, until South Africa comes up with new and more compelling stories, the story of the pass book and how the land was stolen from those who became not only disenfranchised but dehumanised will continue, not only to inform, but also to form the core of the novel in democratic South Africa. Trauma will continue to occupy centre stage – the trauma not only of the victims of apartheid but also that of the perpetrators of the evil. For, let us make no mistake, all South Africans were bonsaied by apartheid – rendered less than they might have been. And that is our story. The story of a land and its people, lost in a fog of evil – for decades. As we slowly, tentatively make our way into the uncharted territory of 'freedom', we cannot but cast our eye back to the bleak wilderness which we are, even now, sloughing off.

We are born into a situation and there is no escape from it; this includes memories of the times – both the blessed memories and the cursed memories; we have no way of choosing. Consciously and unconsciously, one gathers all as one knits oneself into being, using the materials at hand. You can make no other but the self you are, the self who came into that particular world into which you yourself were born, the self who inhabits the particular space you occupy, and has the specific experiences that are yours.

As writers, we write what we know and we know what we have lived. It is in the blood of the story, in the blood of the teller.

PART II
WRITING ABOUT PRESSING ISSUES

Sindiwe Magona delivered 'Address at the Funeral of a Young Woman' – one of the essays in this section – as a speech some years ago at the funeral of a family friend who had died of Aids. It examines the causes of the spread of the virus in South Africa and the impact it had on daily life. The other three essays are newly written pieces that capture Magona's impassioned views on other issues of paramount importance in the current climate: the ever-increasing problem of poverty; the decreasing value assigned to mother tongue; and persistent manifestations of racial tensions within the country. These essays demonstrate Magona's tenacity in addressing these problems head-on and in upending the assumptions that tend to dominate the discourse surrounding these topics.

5.

ADDRESS AT THE FUNERAL OF A YOUNG WOMAN

This is a transcript of a speech that Sindiwe Magona delivered at the funeral of a family friend in December 2002, shortly before her retirement and return to South Africa. In it, she lambasts all those who are to blame in one way or another for the unprecedented spread of HIV (human immunodeficiency virus), which led to South Africa becoming the epicentre of the world's Aids crisis. Her words made such an impact that attendees beseeched her to put the speech in writing. This piece offers one of the clearest examples of the activism that Magona incorporates into her writing.

MY FELLOW AFRICANS, these are bad times, indeed. Daily, sad hordes troop to cemeteries to bury our youth. Custom dictates we bury the dead. However, the acceleration of today's rate of HIV and Aids is alarming, and the age of those dying an abomination. Sadly, we are gathered here today for no different reason. I'm sure I echo what is in the heart of each one here when I say: I wish it were not so.

We have lost a young woman, the youngest of her mother's four girls and the mother of an eight-year-old little girl. Zanele was only thirty years old.

But first, let me begin by expressing my condolences to the bereaved: Dear friends, as the elders say, and have taught us to say: *'Akuhlanga lungehliyo!'*[1] We are all here to shed tears with you in grief, and hope our presence will soften the blow a little.

I would be remiss if I didn't, on behalf of us all, thank this family for what it has done. They have come out publicly; declared their deceased daughter was HIV positive. We thank them for that act of rare and amazing courage; thank them for their leadership.

These days, our sad plight has made us strangers to truth. We have long forsaken truth and chosen the path of appearances and false respectability. As far as I know, this is the first such acknowledgment in Gugulethu. Despite so many of our young people dying daily in unprecedented numbers, we continue to inhabit the house of lies and denial. Yes, Lord, even as we continue to call ourselves Christians, we continue in our wicked lying ways. But this family has decided their loss shall be our gain. Let us be grateful for such bounteous mercy!

Nowadays, even as we frequent cemeteries as though they are leisure palaces, burying not elders but toddlers and young people barely out of their teens, the mouth refuses to speak the outrage. Instead, we all sing the same song: 'No, I don't know where you got that from; all I can tell you, and you'd better believe me because what I'm telling you is the truth – listen: My own child was taken by diarrhoea! Aids? Never! There is nothing of the kind!'

Brother, sister, lies kill. Let us learn a lesson from this family, Christians who practise what they preach. Listen to the words they have asked us to convey to you: 'Our beloved Zanele "succumbed to an illness" – the doctor put this on her death certificate. However, the truth is that she succumbed to an illness only because she was HIV-positive.'

HIV and Aids are indirect killers. But they *are* the killers. Zanele died because her immune system was compromised. What HIV does is strip one's immune system of all protection; it robs the body of its natural ability to defend itself so that it is left with no way of warding off invading bacteria, and that makes the body prone to the slightest assault. A body such as that has no means of protecting or hiding itself, no way of fighting off any illness – whether it is whooping cough, or TB, or a cold, or diarrhoea – whatever and anything – all have an open invitation to further weaken such a body.

The doctor is left to choose the cause of death from an innumerable list of diseases that have enjoyed open house, battering the defenceless and indefensible body at will. These diseases are not called opportunistic for nothing.

In 1990, in New York, I attended a conference organised by a beautiful, spirited, far-sighted, vigorous health worker, Nonceba Lubanga, who hails from Tlokoeng in the Eastern Cape. That is where I first heard the abominable prediction that, by the year 2000, there would hardly be a family in South Africa not affected by Aids or HIV – not one! To me, this sounded outrageous, ludicrous even. You cannot imagine the fear the dreadful prophecy incited in me. I was numbed to the very bone. How could such a thing be possible? How would the country cope with a disaster of such magnitude?

In my fear-induced frenzy, I rolled up my sleeves and sought 'protection' for my immediate family in the form of knowledge: books, pamphlets, flyers, anything that shed light on this disease. Do I not have younger brothers and sisters? Nieces and nephews? Sons and daughters? I was up in arms. 'Here', I said. 'Take these. Read them and be forewarned. Read and digest them that you may live; that you may not die.' Yes, even as I was filled with fear to the point of stupefaction, even then, I realised that 'knowledge is power' – information would be our best armour. Surely, I reasoned, if they know, they will also know how to protect themselves, how to behave in ways that will keep them safe from HIV and Aids.

But I was far from consoled. And my heart was far from stilled, for I knew the folly of youth and the incredible inability of young people to see their own vulnerability. Young people don't die. That is what all youth believe. Knowing that frightening truth, I nevertheless went to the trouble of getting reading materials and sending this home. But each time I returned to South

Africa, I would look at the younger members of my family and ask myself the hard question: which one will it be? Which one, among these, will this disease take? Deep down, I was not convinced I had persuaded everybody in my family of the need for absolute caution, for radical change in sexual conduct – safer sex.

But perhaps there was some element of incredulity even in me. Did I sound the alarm, warn the whole nation? Did I even warn just Gugulethu or even just neighbours and people I knew? Oh, Fear, your second name is Stupidity. Little did I know that families could, and would, lose more than one victim to Aids. Had the doctors at that long-ago conference not said, '... at least *one* victim, per family?' Like a magic charm against evil, I fastened my sight on the *one*. On this false hope, a horrible hope: the worst that could happen was losing one young person per family. I clung to the silly idea as though it were a solemn promise from the Almighty.

Today, all over this country, everywhere black people live in townships, villages, and other predominantly black areas, families bury two or three children, sometimes in the same month. Children of the same mother and father, taken to the cemetery for burial. What else is the poor family to do? The children are dead, and it is customary to bury the dead.

Epidemiologists, doctors, nurses, social workers, demographers and other social scientists tell us that both HIV and Aids are preventable. Yes, these killers are preventable, completely so, in fact.

My fellow Africans, how do our children die of diseases said to be preventable? Where are the parents, that children have become prey to Aids, fair game to what is now commonly known as The Chopper or its Xhosa equivalent *Gawulayo*?[2]

Oh, you do not know how to talk about this to the children?

Shame on you! You have killed your children with your false Christianity and timidity of spirit. Since when, House of Afrika, has nature become something of which one must be ashamed? Since when has a parent become incapable of protecting the child to whom they gave birth? Since when have our bodies and their functions become dirty, things about which we dare not speak?

Oh, my people, have you already forgotten? It was only yesterday that youth was given guidance even in this matter of sexuality. Yes, that was something we did, my brothers and sisters. Before we were converted to Christianity; before we were westernised and civilised, and any other-ised. We were a people who had great caring for our youth, the pride of the nation. The youth was given considered guidance. Young people were shown the way. It was a well-known, accepted fact that there is no opposing nature. But that didn't mean one had to be a victim to nature. No! There was no question of laissez-faire.

Before coming here, I went to a wise old woman in my street, NY 74, in Gugulethu. Mrs Sogiba, whom I called Makhulu Sogiba, confirmed the rumour I had heard, growing up. She said, 'No, during our time, my child, we played. We were young women and young men; we played! But because of what we had been taught we knew full well one did not enter Jerusalem!'

But we left our traditions behind, forsook our ways of doing things, telling ourselves we had seen the light. But that's neither here nor there – I'm not here to delve into the mistakes and errors of our past. Yet I'd like to refer to the famous writer James James Rhanisi Jolobe who said something like: *Isiko limiselwe nje, kuggalwe nto ithile. Kwabona ukuba xa kwenjiwe nje, kuyalunga –* Custom and tradition arise from observations that when things are done in this way, they come out right. But then he went on to say that custom is time-sensitive, that it can change – in fact, *should* be changed or even discarded when the demand arises, when it becomes obvious it no longer serves any useful purpose. If, in time, should the need arise for that custom to be practised again, if it were missed, then it should be brought back, revisited. To me, it is absolutely obvious that the time to revisit this tradition of guiding the young is now. Indeed, I make bold to say that it is long overdue.

There has never been more need of parent-child dialogue, of inter-generational understanding, as there is today. If not now, then when? If not by us, by whom? They say half or fifty percent of the young are at risk. Who will be saved? Who will remain? Is it the remaining fifty per cent that will bear witness to our folly, our timidity, our shame? How can we stand by and watch our nation halved? Halved? And is this the best scenario? There are many who put the survival rate at a lower figure – much lower. We have to – no, we *must* – return to the business of guiding our children on matters of sex. It is a fundamental right, as natural as breathing. This custom is needed again and it is retrievable. You will agree; before was better than this! Before didn't kill. Before didn't have the abomination we have today. Therefore, let us hurry. Back to the Old Ways. Back to Before – before it is too late.

A lot of people and institutions stand condemned. We all stand condemned. For standing by and allowing this epidemic free rein. But first, I blame the church. I sorely fault the church for folding its arms, sealing its lips, and closing its eyes while our children die in droves. The church and the school – two places where most of our young people go, where they congregate to supposedly learn, gain guidance and grow. Where they ought to learn how to live and thrive in this life. But when the matter of sex is raised in church (though in very few churches does this attempt, however feeble, take place), senior members of those congregations are up in arms demanding to know how such filth could be the subject of discussion in church.

Since when is nature an abomination? And how does the church arrive at happily burying the very people it refused to guide and nurture while they still lived? Refused to offer them solace while they suffered the ravage of preventable diseases about which that same church had refused to offer guidance or leadership? Is the church leading or following? If the latter, who is it following? If the former, why are adherents dying in their millions?

And where are the schools in all this? Are schools not places of learning? Is learning not the most important survival tool? What is survival if not knowing how to keep oneself alive? How to make choices that ensure that continuity of life? Almost every young person is, or has been, in the school system. How do our children remain this ignorant of behaviour that would ensure their very survival, despite going through those portals of learning? What is taught at these places of learning? I ask.

You, too, should ask.

Also, I fault the fathers of our children, African men. Beloved fathers, what do you do with these boys when you take them to the bush and bring them back to us proclaiming them men? I had foolishly believed circumcision was more than mere removal of foreskin. I had thought, believed, that this was a time during which a new person was moulded into being. I had thought the ragamuffin, the scoundrel of yesterday, was hewn and smoothed into responsible adulthood. How, then, in today's circumcision rituals, do you bring back rapists? Why is today's circumcision the producer of wicked wolves? Why are our little girls, infants even, as well as grey-haired grandmothers in such dire danger? Why have we, as women, as your mothers, your sisters, your wives, and your daughters, come to find ourselves in perpetual danger, a threatened species? Oh, our fathers, our brothers, our grandfathers and our sons, why have you declared war on Woman – she, who bled you into being? Gave you her blood that you might become?

Men of South Africa, the whole world knows of your wickedness. In the terrible sport of rape, you are leaders! Leaders, in rape! Have you no shame? Have you no hearts? Where is your *ubuntu*?[3] Where your *iintloni*?[4] Where, *intlonipho*?[5] Pray tell us where you have sold your humaneness? Hither will we hurry, that we may go and buy it back, with our very lives, if that is what it will take to restore you to your former wholeness of heart and goodness of spirit.

To that fast-dwindling number of our men – the few we can still call whole, respectable men – I say: Fathers, mind the boys you are raising. Discipline them. Teach them what it means to be a human being – teach them the ways of humanity. Teach them respect, responsibility and self-restraint; those pillars that give meaning to the great gift of being human. Teach them about love. Teach them these things; then will they be men. Fit to live among and with women. Fit for society at large. Fit for life.

But for most of the men here, I am sad to say, you don't qualify for the privilege, the honour, of raising young men. How could you possibly do what I ask, what the African nation so desperately needs, when you have failed to live exemplary lives, failed to live with your wives, the mothers of your sons and daughters, as fitting husbands? How could you possibly be fathers when you have failed to be husbands or moral men? Failed to mete out proper treatment to your families? Failed to live with your families as loving participants in family life, as sons your mothers could be proud they raised; loyal, loving men to your wives or girlfriends, treating them with respect, love and consideration. No, you did not do that. So, all you can be is a terrible example, foul role models of how to live with, how to be with, a woman. All your sons can learn from your example is abuse of women, treating women with disrespect, as when a husband abandons his family, or molesting women, as when a grown man will go after a child young enough to be his own daughter or even his granddaughter – that is molestation.

Sexual relations should be age appropriate. This insensitivity to age is the beginning of the rot, the disrespect of women that leads to atrocious behaviour like rape; the rape of women, the rape of little girls, including infants, and the rape of little boys. What abomination, to be such a terrible example, where the wife and mother is like a newly-hatched chick living in the same coop as a ferocious hungry hawk. What can our young men learn from such fathers? Indeed, is it any wonder that they are in the sorry state in which we find them? This sad spectacle, where men are renowned throughout the world as champion rapists?

Men of South Africa, remake yourselves and mend your ways. Mend the way you treat not only the mother who bore you, but also the woman who bore you your sons and daughters. And mend the way you treat the daughters that spring from your own loins. Mend the ways in which you treat those you profess to love – people who should be under your protection but who, all too often, end up needing to be protected from you. If you are champions at rape, what are the women and children of the country?

Rha-aah![6]

Incest. Promiscuity. Child abuse. Child defilement. Whether it be your own child or the child of another – neighbour, friend, or stranger – African men, when did this horror begin? When did it start? That a full-grown man perceives sexuality in a toddler! Sees an object of sexual desire in an infant in napkins? *Sies!*[7]

Oh, my fathers, my brothers, my sons! Those among you who still have ears, who still have hearts. Open your mouths. Scream out loud against the dastardly crime! Condemn this abomination, this defilement of children! And as far as the African male teacher is concerned, he is a breed that should be culled into extinction. I single out the African male teacher for special condemnation. You are a terrible disgrace to the nation; a double abomination to womanhood. You are among the fortunate few who escaped the full consequences of the plague of apartheid. You were saved through the guidance and perseverance of poor, often uneducated parents and the protection and love of the Ancestors. You were thus chosen so that you would teach the children, the future of the nation; chosen to be yeast to the future of the nation. Instead, it is that very future of the nation you crush under the heel of your sexual deviance. You are predators who destroy whole futures and kill our nation. We send the girl-child to school to be trained, armed, so that she will be of service and value to the nation of which she is an important part, representing, as she does, the perpetuation of the race, the next generation. She is new fruit that will, in due course, mature and bear more fruit. In good time. Meanwhile, this little girl has a childhood to experience, to enjoy, and to negotiate. Your role as her teacher is to help with that most important task: successfully completing the work of childhood in preparation for the rest of her life.

A cock that goes after fledglings is killed and not kept for breeding. Similarly, parents must get rid of predatory teachers – teachers who molest children – whether these be children they teach or children from other schools. Get rid of such teachers! There should be zero tolerance for child abuse of any kind – zero tolerance. Any teacher who molests his young charges is incapable of identifying an appropriate sexual partner. A child can never, under any circumstances, be an appropriate sexual partner. Such a teacher has betrayed a fundamental principle of education – trust.

Dear fellow Africans, love one another. Love with truth in your hearts. Let go of deceit, for today's deceit kills. 'Playboy', 'sugar daddy' – all such words and notions must end. Banish those words from your lips. Expunge them from your vocabulary. Erase them from your consciousness. There are no such people anymore; men who sleep around are killers, *finish en klaar*.[8] Killers. Murderers. *Amagqwirha*.[9] If anything is fuelling the plague of Aids, it is infidelity. I repeat: there are no playboys, only murderers. He who sleeps with multiple partners is nothing but a murderer – just as if he had pointed a gun at his wife or girlfriend. The outcome is the same. Murder. Needless to say, the same goes for a woman who sleeps around. I mention men only because it is a known fact that more men than women are promiscuous. Well, promiscuity has reached epidemic proportions in Africa and it is killing women. More women than men are dying of Aids because for each man who is infected, four or five women are infected. And this is the only place, the only continent in the entire world, where this is true. African women are dying, their children are orphaned, all because African men take it as their God-given right to sleep around, to have more than one woman share their bed. African men are a health hazard, they are sowers of disease, killers of women, orphan-machines who, by their wicked, selfish, mindless actions, depopulate the continent. These men are a curse to the race.

We all have but one shot at life, my dear countrymen. One shot. There are no practice runs. It is up to each one of us to look out for ourselves. Each one of us has to protect herself or himself. The risk of Aids is too serious a threat to one's life to entrust one's safety to another. Bear in mind, when you go to bed with your partner, you go to bed with that person's whole history of sexual engagement. You are not having an encounter with just that one person but with all the people with whom s/he has ever had sexual encounters – and not only them, but with whomever those other people slept with, and so on and so forth. Think about it – how many people have you been intimate with since you became sexually active? If you consider this scenario, of your one-night activity embracing every person your partner has ever been intimate with as well as those who have been intimate with each of those people ... it is quite frightening. A sobering thought.

If, among what might easily be a small army, just one was infected, you are at very high risk of being infected the minute you have unprotected sex with that person or anyone else who has. S/He comes to you with all that history and the significance attached to it. S/He comes to you with that small army and whatever each member carries. Can't you see, isn't it clear then, that carelessness is dangerous? Carelessness kills. Protect yourself. Always, protect yourself. Do not trust another to do the important work of seeing to it that you do not die. That is your job. It is your life.

And to you, my dear sisters, and to you, my beautiful daughters, I say: be careful. Do not pride yourself that you alone have won a man's heart. That he has chosen you. That you have outstripped other women in gaining the attention of a playboy. Beware! Such a victory could be dangerous. You might have just won in a race for the grave.

Abstinence is the only sure way of protecting oneself against HIV. Failing that, the next best thing is *faithfulness*. Neither of these options is easy and it is up to you, the individual, to make the choice. For those in love relationships, there is only one piece of advice. Be loyal. Be faithful. Love your partner so much you will not kill her or him. Love your partner so much that you will protect that person from the vicious plague of HIV and Aids. Be true to your love. Be kind to your love. Keep him or her alive.

Doctors are your friends. Go to the doctor and the clinics. Ask to be tested for these diseases so that you know whether you are well or not. There is no stupidity quite like that of not wanting to know – choosing not to know. Ignorance kills. You won't go to get help if you don't know you need it, will you? How does not knowing help? How can it help? All it does is ensure that your problem goes undetected, untreated, unchecked. All it does is bring you to your death in the quickest possible manner. Why would anyone choose that?

If you test positive, get medical help. Yes, there isn't yet a cure for Aids; but there are drugs that can stall the development of the disease, slow it down, buy you time. If you cannot afford medical treatment, shout – and shout out loudly. That is why countries throughout the world have governments, so that problems such as these can be addressed collectively. Aids is one of our biggest problems in South Africa and the government has to, *must*, respond – and respond in effective ways. Ways that save lives; that keep people from dying. Join with others and raise your voice in protest. From denial to benign indifference, government's response cannot by any stretch of the imagination be seen as addressing the tragedy currently facing the country. But this is *our* government; it is a government of the people. Our cries must reach the ears of our government. Let us send forth a mournful cry. A loud, bold, calamitous howl. These are your children who are dying like flies in a house sprayed with the insecticide Doom. Cry out, loud and clear. Tell the government to do what is right so that millions of lives can be saved. The government is there so that your needs might be answered, your problems faced and, hopefully, be solved. I doubt anyone could say there is a more pressing problem facing our country and our nation today than the Aids pandemic. And I doubt there is one among us who would have the effrontery to claim that she or he will not be touched by the pestilence. Why, then, do we not raise our collective voice and plead with our government, put ourselves at the feet of our government, entreating it to show us mercy, request it to be with us and help us through this, in our hour of direst need? Timidity kills. Silence kills. Dishonesty kills. If we are unhappy or dissatisfied with our government, it is our democratic right to inform the government. Stop fawning; fawning kills. It is not enough to go and stand in long queues every five years to cast our vote. No. Part of our responsibility as a democratic people is to be vigilant, keep our eyes wide open. Without such vigilance, our democracy cannot and will not survive.

We were promised a better life. We were promised we'd be heard. We were even asked to come forward with our concerns, should we have any. We were told we are part of the new deal, part of the new South Africa, part of the rainbow nation. Well, if this is dying, we should loudly shout: *Usan' olungakhaliyo lufel' emb'ekweni.*[10]

The number of people who will perish as a result of Aids far exceeds the deaths that might follow if South Africa were at war, demographers tell us. Were we at war, the powers-that-be would daily address us. When is the last time you heard the president (or any other high-ranking politician) address the nation on this issue? Were we at war, he would have done so on a regular basis. We would have been asked to observe moments of silence. The government would have apprised us of our losses as a nation, given specific numbers of the fallen; it would have advised the nation of ways of combatting the enemy, ways of protecting ourselves against invasion. It would have informed us of what measures to take so as to avoid being overrun by the enemy. And it would definitely have called us up for active military service or service of some other kind. We would certainly have been asked, each one of us, to put our patriotic shoulders to the wheel, to do our bit to save our country.

Why this loud silence? Where is the voice of those who govern us? The nation dying out, the figures of the fallen so high, and with projections this dire, why is there no answering word of advice, no call to arms?

What will future generations say of us? What will they think was the matter with us? What manner of people were we? What were we thinking, they will wonder, that our brothers, our sisters and our children were ravaged so savagely by this disease – ravaged to the point of decimation – with hardly a word from us? Timidity kills.

To the noble family who have shown us the way of the Old, of community, and the Christian way of truth and courage, our deep and grateful thanks are due for your service to the nation. Your wound, you've turned into *iqwili*[11] for the whole nation. To all here present – especially those who have young ones at home or who are themselves young – this noble family has shown exceeding love, of the nation, their nation, our nation. They have given us pamphlets and flyers with information, valuable information on HIV and Aids. We have buttons and badges for sympathisers and supporters to wear, publicly showing support for Aids sufferers and the families of sufferers – spreading knowledge about this scourge so that even those who cannot read might gain insight through such collective efforts. It is now up to us. Up to you and you and you to own this blessing showered upon us by this godly family. It is up to each one of you here to decide whether you came to show sympathy to the bereaved or to get an insider's view of the tragedy for the purpose of gossip, to laugh at these people in their hour of grief. And yet, to me it would appear that even those who came here with scorn and ridicule in their heart must be changed by now – for truth will have changed them, it would have brought about a change of heart even in people such as they. Again, and on behalf of us all, let me express my undying gratitude and fervent admiration for this family for their generosity of spirit. And to show such generosity at a time of grief is not only commendable but also laudable, an example I hope many will follow. It is a gift that will surely save lives.

To conclude: until now, as parents, we have been anxious about our young people, worried that the young women might get pregnant. Brothers and sisters, that was yesterday. Today we worry about the dying of our children, victims ruthlessly felled by the plague and sent to an early grave. Let us reclaim our *ubuntu*; remember our traditions, which we have discarded in unseemly haste, forsaken with alacrity. Let us protect our children by arming them with knowledge. When a child knows that they can protect themselves, they are unlikely to become easy prey to a premature death. Now, who, seeing his house on fire, would turn his back on that house instead of grabbing the nearest container and running to the nearest source of water? The time to act is NOW. Delay and procrastination are deadly. Delay kills. Procrastination kills.

The nearest source of help is with us – with our mouths, mouths that we have far too long kept silent. Speak up! Get involved. Seek and spread knowledge about the pandemic. Join hands with support groups. Stand up and be counted. Failure spells doom for the entire African nation. We keep quiet at our peril. Silence means there will be none left to count. Silence is death. Silence kills. So does shame. That most pernicious killer of all – shame – kills the Aids-sufferer or the person who is HIV-positive long before physical death occurs. Because shame kills the spirit, it dashes hope, exiles the stricken, banishing them to a self-made island that is bleaker, more arid, more God-forsaken even than Robben Island. 'May you die alone!' is one of the most vicious and wicked curses one can lay on the head of another – but this person chooses, is forced by shame to choose, dying alone. Shame is a self-imposed curse, a silent curse. The Aids sufferer, someone who needs and should expect compassion from all of us, shuns the company of fellow human beings and recoils into the private world of despair and fear. Our attaching blame to Aids builds shame in the victims of Aids, and shame gives rise to silence and concealment, which ensures they will not (and cannot) seek treatment. Blame silences the victim. And silence kills.

But that man's or woman's silence, the private agony of their hell – knowing they are dying, and hiding that fact from friend and sometimes even from family – that, my dear brothers and sisters, my sons and daughters, is an indictment of us, the living. A terrible indictment. That a person should be so afraid of our wicked tongues, of our vile insensitivity, our demonic ridicule in their hour of direst need, that they exile themselves, feeling that our compassion will not be there, is a horror that should give us all food for thought. We all stand condemned. Guilty. Never has it been truer than today that for evil to flourish, it is enough for good people to do nothing. But remember, inaction and timidity kill; dishonesty kills; carelessness kills; insensitivity kills. Lying kills. And silence kills.

Today, this family has shown us the way, and it is up to each one of us to take up the challenge. I hope you will leave Zanele's funeral made anew. I pray you will recommit yourselves to be soldiers in the war against Aids. This is the most important task facing our new democracy. It is work whose outcome will make a difference between whether, as a race, we survive or perish.

My sister, my brother, my son and you, my daughter – that work is in your hands. It is up to each one of us to tell ourselves, 'It is up to me!' and to do what must be done.

Thank you for your attention. Now, let's go out there, back to our homes and places of work and worship – and fight the good fight. The struggle continues!

6.
DO NOT CHOOSE POVERTY

This essay spells out in detail the personal story that Sindiwe Magona references again and again in her writing: her dramatic escape from the extreme poverty she was born into as a black South African woman in 1943. She leans heavily upon this origins narrative not to castigate those in unfortunate circumstances but to inspire them to reject the assumption that the poor inherently lack the agency to improve their lives.

MANY OF THE world's poor are born into poverty. Some escape, many do not. Tragically, many do not only not escape poverty but actually sink deeper and deeper into the quagmire. However, most, if not all, have a fighting chance to escape poverty. Take it from me, you *can* escape poverty. I know, because I did.

I was born poor. That is true of most people my age group, born black in apartheid South Africa or before. Black-black[1] Africans were not recognised as citizens of South Africa, their birth country. Apartheid South Africa was governed by white people, governed with the sole purpose of legally barring all those not white-skinned from meaningfully participating in the economy of the country – the darker, the further the push away from being a person who experienced a life worth living. Yes, even oppression apartheid implemented according to rank: white best; coloured next; black crushed to the ground. Black-black people didn't even have identity numbers. An ID number means you are counted as a human being, a member of a society, with a numerical value in the census. Black Africans were not counted – not as South Africans. Which is why describing the pass or *dompas*[2] as an identity document, as some are wont to do, is incorrect. The pass book was a reference book in that it provided a number in reference to a black body being in a certain geographical or urban area, legally, for the purpose of residence (if that body qualified for this 'right'), and/or the employment of a black body by such and such – this last, always and only a white body or organisation comprising a group of white bodies. Residence and employment, the first to serve the second, were the two criteria. Visits, as for a funeral or wedding, were of very short duration – never more than three weeks; vacation from work, normally a month (minus travel time, three weeks) is all one was permitted. The reference book had a seven-digit number called a reference number, with the prefix M for *man*/male or V/F for *vroumens*/female. An identity number identified the person as a citizen of South Africa. White, coloured, Asian and Indian were all citizens – but not 'Bantu'.[3] The laws of the country selectively ensured white wealth and black oppression and, in that way, artificially created a poverty-black nexus. Despite appearances, poverty is not the natural status of blackness, and in South Africa it was created and determined by law.

However, as already stated, despite that enormous handicap, some did manage to escape dire poverty – as I did. I am not suggesting escaping from poverty is easy; if it were, everyone in that situation would have left it already. To put it differently, no one would linger too long in poverty, for poverty's other name is Misery – yes, with a capital M. However, because of poverty, more people of colour than white people are poor, and because historical social engineering ensured that outcome in South Africa, most of the poor have been and still are black people. Poverty has, thus, come to be associated with skin colour. A fallacious assumption.

Poverty is not your skin. It is not your eyes. It is not you. You may have been (and probably were) born into poverty. But you do not have to be poor all your life. Just think, you may live to be eighty or ninety. That is a long, long time. Too long to spend in misery; and, believe me, poverty is nothing if not pure, unadulterated misery. I know – been there, done that.

I grew up poor, but I had no idea we were poor. Our parents did their utmost to hide the fact that we were poor. And since every child in the location where I grew up had the same living standards, how could I have known that this was not the natural order of things? We children, all of us, thought we were just fine. Everybody went to school barefoot. I was never in a class where every child had all the books the teacher said we needed. I had no idea such a possibility was the norm elsewhere ... in the same, very same country in which I was growing up.

I had a very happy childhood. My parents worked hard and sent me to school – primary and secondary and then teacher-training school.

I was the first in my family to qualify for a job! Nineteen years of age.

But the same year I started teaching, I fell pregnant. I lost my job and was put on a two-year probation. That was the rule then for unmarried women teachers who fell pregnant. Schoolgirls were simply expelled if they fell pregnant. In quick succession, there was baby number two, and marriage in anticipation of that; baby number three arrived hardly a year later. By then, horror of horrors – abandonment.

The second volume of my autobiography, *Forced to Grow*, begins: 'I was a "has been" at the age of twenty-three. Sans husband, I was the mother to two little girls and expecting my third child – as it turned out, a son. He was born ... four months after his father had left us.' Twenty-three – and I plunged from poverty to destitution.

Remember, I was a non-citizen in the country. Among other things, I could not access government help for my children. The South African Child Welfare Society did not cater to 'Bantu' children. Because I knew this, it never even occurred to me to approach that organisation and apply for assistance. I was five when trains became segregated – yellow boards on windows, marked WHITES ONLY. That sign would appear in the doorways of the post office, hospitals, buses, beaches … therefore, I did not approach the South African Child Welfare Society, even though I had three children and we were destitute. It would not have helped our situation to get myself arrested.

I took stock of my situation: I had brought disgrace on the name of my family, husbandless, with a whole carriageful of children. No longer teaching, the sacrifices my parents had made were nullified by the bad choices I had made. Shame was my second name. Shame and anger filled me – but they also fuelled me.

Society, I knew, did not fault the father who had abandoned his children; I was the laughingstock, the frigid woman who could not keep her man. What little education I had did not help me in my hour of dire need. Male teachers were never 'punished' for impregnating a woman not married to them. Blame was my game: my husband, society, and the stupid, evil apartheid government.

Then, finally, it dawned on me: my anger was misdirected, wasted; it served no useful purpose. The people to whom it was directed didn't even know my name – why would they care if I was angry at them? And the one who did know my name, cared even less. Had he cared, he wouldn't have left, would he?

Waste of my energy.

I realised that the only person who mattered in the equation, the only person against whom I ought to turn my anger was none other than me.

Why?

Because I am the only person I can direct. The only person who can do my bidding, without fail.

What needed doing? Needed doing as a matter of urgency? By none other but me. Seeing to the welfare of my poor children, of course.

Thank God for my parents. They were my role models. I looked back and saw what they had done for their children – sent us all to school. Peasants who, between the two of them, had not even one certificate of education, had somehow managed to give us a fair chance at a reasonably good life – a much better life than they had ever had, or could have had.

My children deserved that, at the very least. It would not be unreasonable for them to expect more of me. I, a qualified primary school teacher, was in a far better position to give them that than my parents had been.

Shame was still there. But now it was shame at allowing myself to waste more time, crying over spilt milk instead of looking forward – mapping a way out of the muddy hole into which I had plunged myself.

Mea culpa! But, hey! I will save myself – *must*!

I vowed to work hard, very hard, to salvage my life – for the sake of my children.

The only jobs available for the likes of me were working in white people's homes. I did that – for four years. However, I had a plan. I was not going to be a domestic worker for the rest of my life. What is more, neither of my daughters would ever be a domestic worker and my son would never be a garden 'boy'. Domestic work is a job, and I don't look down on it. But, for me, it was a stepping stone.

I chose not to stay in domestic work for life.

Choice is life because the choices we make determine the life we live. I had made bad choices, therefore, from 23 on, I had work to do – digging myself out of a hole, out of destitution. At the same time, I had to be mindful I didn't dig myself even deeper into that hole. It happens.

No more children.

Children cost a lot of money: think of all the things they need – and understandably expect to receive from their parents. This points to something many people, especially the poor, overlook: planning for the wherewithal needed to care for children before they arrive. I had had my children without any planning; the least I could then do, so as not to make an already bad situation worse, was to make sure I did not produce another child.

After seeing to that, next came the idea to improve my qualifications, to make myself more marketable/employable as a teacher. Taking note of the scarcity of highly qualified teachers in the Western Cape at the time, I realised that I would secure a teaching post with ease were I to get a matric certificate.

Decision: study for matric.

Problem: where is the money to come from?

Solution: spend less of what you earn, and save for your education.

You did not have any wages not so long ago. Now you do. Don't get used to 'needing' all you earn. Save for tomorrow! Getting that matric would improve our situation immensely, whereas using up all the money on today's needs was a sure way of aborting a rosy tomorrow. I chose the promise of a rosy tomorrow.

Those two choices, limit the number of children and further studies, were sturdy staves in my walk away from destitution and towards freedom.

I made those choices less for the love of them, but more because I hated what I had become. Twenty-three, the perfect product all black people were engineered to be by apartheid, and I hated it. Hated it so much. Determination gave me wings, and once again I vowed I would not linger long in domestic service, and nor would my children be relegated to a life of servile work.

In two years flat, studying by correspondence, I matriculated. In the course of that time, I had been recruited for a teaching job half-way through my matric studies. Passing the final exams was the affirmation I in fact needed. And, as the saying goes, 'Nothing succeeds like success'. Now no longer in domestic service, and teaching at a secondary school, my appetite had been whetted. I began studies for A-Levels, again by correspondence, this time through London University. That was affirmation unparalleled. Surprised at my own success, my bludgeoned confidence was building itself up. That is healing, a possibility waiting for anyone who has lost their way as I had. But healing or mending begins with that first step. Agency is the name of the game in life. Nothing beats it, and nothing can replace it.

In a flash, that leap into the future I had perceived but dimly a few years before materialised so swiftly, so unexpectedly, it took even me by surprise. But it whetted my appetite for even more.

After I completed the A-Levels, in one year, I registered for a Bachelor of Arts degree through Unisa (the University of South Africa). That took five years, by correspondence. All that studying amounted to eight years. That may seem like a huge slice out of someone's life. It is. But I do not regret it a bit. What is the alternative? What more could I have done with the eight years? More domestic work? Continue hoping to get a teaching post? As a married woman, the possibility was very slim. For five years after I was abandoned by a man I called My Husband, I stayed away from men; I was in no hurry for more trouble.

Meanwhile, my life and those of not only my children but my parents and my siblings – all younger than me and still in school – were faring much better, thanks to the improvement in my own status. From teaching at Fezeka Secondary School in Gugulethu, Cape Town, I took up an attractive offer to work for the Cape City Council, more than trebling my teacher's salary! I then left that job for a position with the National Union of South African Students (Nusas),[4] and then followed another, and another. The last job I had in South Africa was teaching at Herschel Girls School.[5] The five years I spent there was the longest period I'd taught in any school … for good reason. My salary had nothing to do with my race classification, skin colour or gender! To say nothing of the physical conditions. The enthusiasm of the teachers as well as the learners, their conscientious dedication, developed me both as a teacher and a human being; all the people there, including clerical staff and ordinary workers, were gracious, thereby blending with the institution's buildings and grounds.

I had fallen on hard times in my early twenties. But because I'd consciously made a decision to run away from poverty and had acted upon it, taken the necessary steps towards the realisation of the desired outcomes, I had succeeded. Nobody loves poverty. Nobody decides to park themselves there for life. However, unless one's hatred of poverty is accompanied by a conscious decision to get up and go, to leave poverty behind, followed up by concrete action, nothing shifts – nothing can shift. The first shift is deciding to flee from poverty, followed by brave bit-by-determined-bit steps, mindful not to look back or slide back into the hole you're leaving. In short, to escape poverty, you must flee it – that is active action, not wishful thinking but bold steps that ensure the desired outcome.

The steps I had taken eventually enabled me to get a scholarship to do a master's degree at Columbia University in New York; I thought I had reached the ceiling of what I could expect in life. It was at Columbia School of Social Work that I first encountered the term 'the working poor'. My eyes opened. Yes, I got the formal education at Columbia University, but I got a whole lot more. Fellow students took me on tours, to Harlem and the South Bronx. I had never seen such desolation in South Africa. Yes, in the Cape Town area we had what we called 'Bergies' – homeless people who holed up in the mountains. However, back then, these seemed few and far between – not the nation-wide deluge one sees these days, some thirty years post the first democratic election of 1994. It was in the United States that I began to better understand the engineered nature of my poverty back home in South Africa. I felt for my parents. My father, who had slaved all his life within a system where failure was inbuilt. But I also learnt there were other ways of engineering poverty … and, yes, skin colour played a part in that.

During my time in the US, I quickly learnt that African Americans were over-represented in the poverty category of the population – just like 'Bantus' in South Africa. However, the African Americans were far more au fait with their plight, with the underlying causes and its history. What is more, they had been doing something about it for many years already with social groups like the National Association for the Advancement of Colored People, which had prominent leaders as members.

The arts featured their history, including that of poverty. A comedian, showing no qualms at all, shouted into the mike at one show: 'Why do poor people stay poor?' Pause. Then he answered his own question: 'Because they keep on doing what poor people do!' Another pause as the audience reacted and he nodded his assent before further elaborating: 'Yes, ma'an! RICH

PEOPLE STAY RICH BECAUSE THEY DO WHAT RICH PEOPLE DO – INVERSELY: POOR STAY POOR THE SAME WAY ... they be doing what poor people do ... on and on and on. How d'you think they gonna change, then? Damn! They stay poor! Amen!'

This kind of explanation, and the way it was given, surprised me at first. Offensive? Blaming the victim? Let's just say it was not something I would have had the courage or chutzpah to voice out loud. Thinking about it later, however, I began to see the logic of it. Brash? Yes. But, also true. Very true! That 'insulting' skit showed me, or reminded me of, the reality that is role modelling, something we humans do either with or without intent. The younger members of society, children, pick up behaviours and attitudes from the adults they grow up around. How is a child to learn of thrift if it is never practised at home or in the community? Ditto for family planning – or anything else, for that matter. Ambition? Clear-sightedness about planning for 'when I finish school'? In the homes of the poor, children seldom, if ever, witness 'planning' of any kind. What abounds is wishful thinking, blaming the oppressor or misfortune, rather than deciding what to do to change one's situation or circumstances. We live habituated lives, and the role modelling is often more poisonous than helpful, let alone stimulating.

In the US, I found the groups working for black upliftment admirable. In some of what they advocated, I saw a little of my own path, what I had done – was doing, hence my sojourn at Columbia. But I also saw more – much more than what I had done. I saw the possibility of combatting poverty back home by doing what I saw being done in the US: community upliftment.

And, as luck would have it, I was getting the requisite training too. Community Organisation was the platform I selected when I enrolled at the School of Social Work. I planned to come back and do community work. I had had a taste of that, and loved it, when I worked for the Cape City Council. I was certain that that work experience, combined with the training I got at Columbia, would provide me with a job back in South Africa, and I would be involved in community upliftment work, which had begun to emerge even before I left for Columbia University. I was very, very hopeful regarding my prospects.

However, life happens, and the best-laid plans go flippy-flop. I was wrong. The Columbia experience led to a job at the United Nations (UN). And that is where the former domestic worker who was a has-been at age twenty-three spent the next twenty-five years of her working life. Working at the UN headquarters in New York. By the way, that is also where her three children, no longer very little by this time, also lived. During her UN years, they completed high school in the US and each one graduated from college – an accomplishment that could barely have been hoped for back in South Africa.

The UN experience, a marvellous opportunity, was nonetheless a learning curve. Growth is, or can be, perplexing; it is not always comfortable. That international organisation employs human beings. Human beings are nothing if not complex. Believing the UN to be a champion for the oppressed, I was not a little taken aback to find myself not treated in any way as special. Remember the poor education of which I was a product, and about which much was spoken in UN General Assembly debates? Well, don't think that when I was inept or found lacking in the most basic skills, everyone around me understood. My apartheid background provided no 'Let's cut her some slack' attitude from colleagues or supervisors. My performance of any task proved, as it should, how fit/unfit I was for the job. I had no quarrel with that. But the discovery that, even while the world condemned South Africa, as it should, this did not automatically translate to empathy for the 'oppressed' individual was quite a shock to me. Lesson learned: don't bank on being anyone's *foeitog*.[6] If you need something, get it for yourself. The realisation led to understanding, and I am eternally grateful. That was a huge part of my journey into personal and professional growth, as I began to see that this is what 'equal treatment' actually meant. I realised that being given leeway to remain an underperformer would have been not only injurious to my personhood, but insulting as well. It was bad enough I had grown up groomed to expect less of myself; having others expect less of me, especially people and places I held in high esteem, would have been the death of me as far as personal growth is concerned. I learnt a lot at the UN about that, becoming increasingly a 'better you', and, what is more, engendering that spirit in others. It was an environment both inspired and inspiring.

On my retirement, I returned to my pre-UN plans. During apartheid, I had trained to do community work, and my excitement grew at the thought that I would now be doing that work in the new South Africa. Instead of working against the apartheid government, I would be working in conjunction with the new government, as community building had to be at the forefront of what was happening in South Africa. My people, my nation, was in sore need of help. It needed help. It needed all hands on deck – surely?

I got myself so excited, I actually sought help in mapping out a thirty-year plan for community upliftment, to overturn poverty. I returned, fully convinced I would be of value – would be welcomed, embraced and encouraged to join the battle before us all: working to heal a broken people. But my return did not turn out exactly as I planned, as my hopes of building a large-scale programme to assist in the education of the nation's youth was not met with the enthusiasm I had expected. But it did begin my journey of using my writing to create change, which I have been on ever since. Through my words, this 'has-been' is working to help those who consider themselves incapable of escaping poverty to get the traction they need to start the process of creating change in their lives.

I am exceedingly grateful for the life I have. I get complimented by my childhood friends and former colleagues and others who know me from church and my neighbourhood, on my achievement. I accept the compliments. However, I always point out I did not do it alone. It has been a journey in the company of others, with helping hands and generous and encouraging spirits. Also, making the decisions I made and undertaking the steps and follow-up was no walk in the park. But, taking everything into account, the alternative would have been far, far worse – grinding poverty, the living death that is the plight of millions of people here, in our beautiful country, South Africa.

One may be born into poverty, and no one can blame a child for being in that situation. However, one does not have to live all one's life in poverty. Poverty is not only unpleasant, it is unhealthy, it is ugly, it is all the things no one wants. No one would choose to be poor. However, as a grownup, one should do everything in one's might, undertake every possible and legal endeavour, to get out of Country Poverty.

Choose to *leave* poverty!

Do not choose poverty, for poverty is death. Poverty kills. The poor die young. The quality of life for the poor is abysmal.

It is not easy to do the hard work that enables one to escape from poverty. But staying in poverty is much, much harder.

When you fail to choose to leave poverty, you choose to stay. You choose poverty. Yes, you may not say it out loud. You may not even say it softly to yourself or think it. However, you are choosing poverty if you don't make that crucial choice to leave it and then figure out the steps you need to take to make that happen. And get excited thinking about the prospects … what you are about to do and what it means to you and your family. *See* it happen. Picture it. Picture yourself in that 'future' space. That is called dreaming, and, as the saying goes, 'Where there are no dreams, people simply perish!'

My life is not unique, but it could be used as an example. Nobody escaped apartheid – not totally, at any rate. Yes, we are all scarred. However, it is a matter of degree. I share my life because I believe it is a gift to me and could be a gift to another, or to others who are in the dark space that I was in all those decades ago. That, and the fact that I come from very humble beginnings, means I am the same as the majority of black-black and poor South Africans. Take a leaf out of my book, I say. It is possible. I did it, and so can you! All it takes, all you need, is your own God-given abilities or talents, and bitter hatred of poverty, coupled with a fierce determination to leave it, abandon it, divorce it … and go get yourself the perfect life – perfect, for you.

Everyone deserves their best life. Those who go for it, work for it, will find there is a lot of help along the way. But help will not come and wake you up; it is up to you to get up and find it.

7.
CRY, THE BELOVED LANGUAGE

This essay, which is based on a lecture Sindiwe Magona delivered in 2014 at a conference in South Africa, articulates her beliefs about the importance of indigenous languages and the damage that is done through the estrangement from mother tongue. Just as Alan Paton warns in his famous novel[1] of the danger that the apartheid regime poses for the nation, Magona anticipates the disintegration of the society should mother tongue continue to be sidelined or, worse, blatantly denied.

THE THEME OF this conference – 'Reclaiming Our Heritage through Language'[2] – leads me to believe that we recognise that, as a nation, we were left something by our progenitors: heritage. I make bold to say that this belief goes beyond mere recognition to include the realisation that this heritage, this inheritance is worthy – hence the intention to reclaim. In short, we admit to the fact of having been left something worthy, which we no longer have, and which we intend to get back.

What is it we have lost, or think we have lost? How did we lose whatever it is we have lost? Was it taken from us, stolen, or did we lose it through neglect – our neglect? Or did we simply throw it away? Did we go to sleep and let it die an unmourned death, without even being aware it was dying or had died?

Since we declare that we intend to get back that which we have lost, and to do that by means of language, it seems to me it would be right and proper to first examine the instrument by means of which we mean to accomplish our goal. Thus, for the main part, I shall attempt to do exactly that – examine that instrument. Having chosen language as the instrument we shall use in this most important task, have we looked at it closely? Have we examined it to evaluate its fitness for the job? I assume we have. Surely we have, for what warrior would dare set out to do battle without having first ascertained that their weapon was up to the challenge? Our weapon, according to the title, is language – to be specific, isiXhosa, the language of *amaXhosa*, the Xhosa people. But is isiXhosa ready for the task?

First, however, what, precisely, is language? With the aid of the two or three dictionaries I have at my disposal at home, I have come up with a definition: Language is the instrument human beings use to communicate thoughts and feelings. This is something that our Ancients did, and did satisfactorily. In modern times, language, including isiXhosa, was reduced to representation by means of symbols – and so we have written language. Through such means, language is preserved and perfected. Moreover, we are hereby able to trace trends and developments in language. We are able to recognise norms and standards, as well as detect deviations – whether these be the result of progress, neglect or being birthed by not only indifference but outright hatred of our mother tongue. Hopefully, whatever deviations might occur in isiXhosa will come from the deliberate acts of the present caretakers of our heritage, language. Of course, the aforesaid presupposes that one cares enough about that language to do the requisite work: safeguarding and monitoring it; protecting and nurturing it.

There lies the rub, however: you cannot protect what you do not love; you cannot love what you do not understand; you cannot understand what you do not know; you cannot know that with which you are not in contact – *intimate contact!*

Here I would like to use an example with which most of us, I dare say all of us, are familiar: falling in love. The prerequisite for that universal human phenomenon is proximity. You cannot fall in love with someone you have not met, someone you do not understand – someone with whom you have had no dealings or whom you do not particularly like. That begs the question: How intimate *are* you with your mother tongue? What is the title of the latest novel published in that language? Who is the author? Have you read the novel? Do you know the publisher? Is it a reputable publisher? What reviews has the novel had? Were they favourable or not? When is the last time you gave a book in your mother tongue as a gift to someone in your family or to a friend? What are the best children's books in your language? The most widely read? Can you name the top twenty? Have you read any of those? Can you name six writers of children's books who write in your mother tongue?

It is commonly believed that children deserve to have books written by people who look like them; who draw characters that look like them; who tell stories that the children are familiar with; who paint scenes likely to be found in homes like theirs, whether the children are *amaXhosa*, rural or urban, rich or poor, highly educated or not. Our children deserve to see their world in print before they venture forth to Brazil, Yugoslavia, Finland – or Mars! My children need books written in isiXhosa, written *ngamaXhosa!*[3]

Language is part of our culture, it is part of our identity, and it comes to us through learning which, scientists tell us, begins *in utero.* Could that be why one of the languages everyone, anywhere in the world speaks, is called 'Mother Tongue'? There are people fortunate enough to be multilingual, but very few will speak the acquired language or languages with the same degree of proficiency as that of a mother-tongue speaker. Given this, one would think it would be obvious that one's mother tongue should be a source of pride, but in South Africa this does not seem to be the case. Indeed, black South Africans are doing a harm to themselves far beyond what apartheid managed to do. Apartheid, for whatever reason, left our languages intact. But now that we are free, we are busy de-tonguing ourselves – doing to ourselves what slavery did to African slaves in America and, sadly, to their descendants, African-Americans. Slaves, dragged across the seas, with many dying along the way and dumped into icy oceans, were deliberately separated from those who spoke their language. Today, their descendants have no other language apart from that of their former enslavers, their mother tongue excised from their psyche – from their very souls. Forever and irredeemably lost.

The slave owner had a system. He took the trouble to identify the slave through language and then embarked upon a course of action designed to kill that crucial aspect of his property's identity – language. By separating the slaves along language lines, the slave owner ensured that their languages would fall into disuse. Language is a social tool, something one uses in the course of interacting with others. By this act of deliberate disinheritance, the slaves – who had already lost their freedom – lost their languages. This sad history proves that continuous engagement and use is necessary not only for the survival but also for the growth of language.

Today, certainly in South Africa, African schoolchildren *choose* their mother tongue. Freedom has gone to our heads! How can you *choose* your mother tongue? Is it not a given? In my view, language is as integral a part of one's being, one's identity, as skin colour. Can anyone choose his or her skin colour? What, then, does the need to deliberately disinherit ourselves, lose our languages, indicate? What does this suggest about the psychological state of a people? Is this phenomenon healthy? If not, why do parents allow their children to turn their backs on their mother tongue? Why are we doing to ourselves what the slave owners did to the slaves? Why are we disinheriting ourselves? Surely, this is disrespect for our heritage, for what our Ancestors bequeathed us? And why does the government allow such abomination? Indeed, we are a sad and sorry lot.

Compare this to the story of the Afrikaner. When the Afrikaner came into power, he ensured that his language, his culture, his tribe thrived. There was a flourishing of the arts in Afrikaans, a burgeoning of education. To this day, the monuments of that blossoming stand, strong and proud. Without such a spirit of self-love, there would have been no University of Stellenbosch, no NB Publishers,[4] no pioneering heart transplant. The Barnard Brothers,[5] Chris and Marius, sons of a Dutch Reformed Church clergyman who was far from wealthy, both became medical doctors. The women's group, Die Suid-Afrikaanse Vroue Federasie, put their limited savings together, rather like a stokvel.[6] Their aim was to ensure that no Afrikaner child who showed promise was deprived of an education through lack of money.

The Afrikaner did not wait for the British – their former oppressor – to uplift them. They did it themselves – which is, in one sense, exemplary. But I do not in any way applaud the Afrikaner for forgetting the cruelty of his oppression and going on to ensure the oppression of another. No. I am referring to his use of the freedom he had gained for himself to ensure that his tribe would benefit from it. Importantly, this tribe was not limited to his immediate family, friends and cronies or his own village. It benefited his tribe in its entirety, with none left behind. That is what I applaud, for that is what ensured the survival and growth of his language, Afrikaans. Afrikaans literature has a loyal readership, and is seemingly the most widely-read language in the country. Even if that is not the case, what is certain is that Afrikaans authors are the envy of others – some are even able to live off their royalties!

I doubt that the same could be said about authors who write in other indigenous languages. Apart from the odd exception, authors who write in the indigenous languages of South Africa are fated to work at their craft part-time, subsidising their writing with a more 'serious' job. You will seldom find a book written in our indigenous languages in the top ten or top twenty of children's books in South Africa. To reach that position, a writer needs a loyal readership. Do we have that? Do those of us who write for children in isiXhosa, isiZulu, isiSuthu, etc., have loyal readerships? The answer is an unequivocal no!

Languages can die. For language is a dynamic, living thing which, if neglected long enough, will wither and eventually disappear. By allowing our children to choose whether or not to use their mother tongue, by neglecting our writers and the books written in our languages, we show disrespect to those languages. But the more painful fact is the disrespect we show to our Ancestors, our progenitors, the elders who left us language – and then we wonder why we are in the state we are in. How can we be in a healthy, robust state, a thriving state, when we have effectively turned our backs on ourselves?

And, please, do not give me that 'We were taught to hate ourselves and all things that are essentially us by our oppressors'. For, if you know that much, what is your response? What good is this knowledge if it serves not to so enrage you that you show your oppressor what you are made of? It seems to me that it cannot be my duty, as an oppressed person, to further the aims of my oppressor by doing his work for him. What it all boils down to is this: we do not respect our languages because we do not respect ourselves, that is, we have a low regard for what is the essence of our very being. Without self-respect, all else is of little or no avail.

Respect for one's self, for the other, and for the environment – this is the living embodiment of what we have inherited. You (the self), living in the midst of innumerable others, living through the kindness and abundance of the environment – the only real thing you will leave posterity that is of genuine worth. You may leave diamonds and gold, but what are all such material things without potable water? Without arable land? Without clean, life-supporting air? The environment or Mother Earth and all there is on and in and above her – known and unknown, visible and invisible – is *there*. She is there, supporting life without prejudice or favouritism – and all she asks of you is respect. Language is the instrument, the key instrument we can use to instil these and other values. It is the instrument that can help us and all humanity to live in harmony in the world in which we dwell, and posterity too.

One of the most important battles facing humanity today is that of saving our Earth. If our language – our mother tongue – does not begin to address issues of pollution, recycling, and global warming, issues crucial to the survival of humanity, of what use is our ability to communicate? Where are the books, the songs, the dances, the theatre, the films about how we human beings, through our careless and wanton actions, are destroying Mother Earth? Our eyes need to be wide open. Earth is slowly but surely dying. *Wafa umhlaba sibukele!*[7] Yet we have not come up with corresponding words for what is happening. Indeed, we are busy killing off even words that might be of some help. What has happened to words such as *ihlazo, inyala?*[8] We don't even mildly query *'Uthi wenzani?'*[9] Never mind bolder demands such as: *'Baph' abantu? Babephi n'abantu?'*[10]

Similarly, where are the essays, the poems, the plays documenting the post-apartheid era in the indigenous languages of this country? The story of South Africa with its growing shame and disaster? To date, the brilliance of the Zulu writers Mazisi Kunene[11] and the Dhlomos[12] are hidden in plain view from other indigenes. What of the philosophy left us by the poet laureate of *amaXhosa* and indeed, the entire nation, S.E.K. Mqhayi?[13] Where, in our education and discourse, is the wisdom of A.C. Jordan?[14] Why is it that we cannot do in our own country what European Literature manages to achieve? French writers are not unknown in England, and vice-versa. When will South African authors who write in mother tongue cross language borders instead of being 'script-locked' in their respective tongues, as writers of the African continent continue to be in their own countries? Not too soon, I dare say, since they are still only read by speakers of whatever vernacular they use; we are all the poorer for it, for we have no idea what wealth may lie in their works. Linguists could help dissolve these language borders, they and other language specialists. If only they would take up the challenge!

What our beautiful country needs, as a matter of self-nurturing, is a broad-based, diverse literature. Literature abounds in this country – in all its forms: oral storytelling; drama; film; song and dance; games, including word games; novels, short stories, poetry and essays. But all this wealth is held in apartheid fashion, divided according to linguistic groupings. This calls for translation galore so we can, finally, share in and partake of one another's feast of literary delights. Write. Write. Write! Thereafter, translate, translate! A whole national and, indeed, continental undertaking, sure to facilitate, aid and encourage our becoming more and more familiar with one another. In these times of globalisation, with boundaries becoming more and more fragile and porous, this is not only something that might help; it is a necessity. Let alone the exciting prospect of job creation: a whole enterprise of translation workers doing something they enjoy. The editors, the publishers of works in indigenous languages ... thriving, at last.

But the current state of our languages does not inspire much confidence that they might be effective instruments in waging any battle at this moment in time. We need to sharpen our spears – and if that spear is language, then we need to sharpen language. One has only to look at government notices, examination papers, the media and published books to see that isiXhosa, for one, is in dire need of reform. Also, we will need good editors. It is my humble belief, if we are sincere in our desire to reclaim our inheritance, that we should first reclaim our language. When she has been remade, even perfected up to a point, she will be a worthy instrument with which to reclaim our full inheritance, our birthright.

8.
WE ARE ALL RACISTS!

In this essay, Sindiwe Magona articulates little discussed aspects of race revolving around race hate and the feelings of inferiority engendered by racial hierarchies. Her free flow of ideas provides far-reaching and personal insights into the harm caused by racial discrimination and the need for people of all races to rise above the insidious discourse that typically characterises discussions of race.

THE DEBATE AROUND race in South Africa today is stymied by accusations of racism levelled by the right as well as the left. What these charges essentially do is shut down conversation. In this essay, I will try to open up the discussion by making three claims, which I will follow up with a stream of thoughts that I am still in the process of refining. Some of what I explore here will, no doubt, make a lot of people uncomfortable, but I hope my reflections will allow us to move beyond the current moment of mud-slinging.

Claim #1: We are all racists! In saying this, I am redefining racism to mean simply paying attention to physical differences – a natural consequence of our diversity. But racialism is something else altogether. It occurs when certain attributes are assigned to those differences – which inevitably leads to negative thinking about another group and negative actions against said group.

I am a racist.

That is a fact. I admit: I am a racist. That is not to say I am proud of the fact – yet nor am I ashamed of it. But before you go gasping and condemning, let me tell you something we can't deny: you, too, are a racist. We are all racists. Simply put: all human beings are racists – an indisputable fact. Deny it if you like, but that won't change the matter. All humanity is racist. As long as people have eyes, and skin has a certain colour, no way can one not notice skin colour – not notice the different tones of it. Skin Colour Difference is real. It is vividly visible. Seeing that difference means we are racist.

There is nothing peculiar about this phenomenon, for it is simply part of human life – part of the diversity that human life manifests. A gorgeous diversity, by the way. And noticing that, inevitable as the act is, it is neither a crime nor a sin – merely a part of our existence, inescapable. And our admitting to being racist does not automatically make us racialists. That comes with the choice we make regarding what to do about the difference we see and cannot but see, unless we are visually impaired. Racialism happens when we attach value to skin colour – that is the demarcation line between racist and racialist, we have become racialistic when we do that.

A case in point: becoming aware of difference of skin colour happened very early in my life – even before I had started school. Before my family left the village of my birth, in the Transkei, and went to live in a tin-shack or pondokkie location[1] in Retreat, near Cape Town, I knew there were people 'with no colour' – *abelungu*. That was all that seeing those strange people told me – they were different because they had no colour in their skin. Nothing wrong with that but, nevertheless, it was disconcerting, if only because it was first time I'd found myself confronted with the phenomenon.

Yet as I grew older, something was added to the visible difference of skin colour. I don't remember Mama or Tata ever sitting me down and 'schooling' me into believing this or that about *abelungu*. However, I soon picked up 'attitude' or 'beliefs' attached to having a no-colour skin. Most of what I picked up was not directed at me per se, but it planted itself nonetheless in my mind.

I soon got to 'know' that all *abelungu* were rich beyond belief; they employed black people; they were unkind to the workers they employed; they did as little work as possible, but ensured much was done under their supervision, using black men and women to do that work. They paid themselves lots of money and paid black people as little as possible. That was because they had power, for the government favoured them and oppressed black people.

A child picks up a whole lot of knowing about the world into which she or he has recently come. All a child will ever know she will learn after she is born. We all come into the world innocent of any knowing. My home, the location where I lived, was a home away from home for a few women and a large number of African men who went to Cape Town seeking employment, leaving their families far away in the village we had left. There was a lot of gossip, a lot of grumbling, seldom any praise for *abelungu* – the masters and madams who employed these men and women. Grownup talk, grumbles about what happened at work, laws that *abelungu* inflicted on 'us', and a host of other inferences.

This often became part of our play as children, part of our make-believe world. Yes, some of us would play at being 'Medems' while others would be 'girls', as maids – grownup women – were often called. Instead of using the woman's name, her 'medem' would often refer to 'my girl'; similarly, a black man was called 'boy' by any white person or child old enough to speak.

By the time I started school, aged six, I was pretty clued up on what *abelungu* did to us, treating us unfairly. At the same time, I had a hard time differentiating between the different 'races' – white, coloured, Asiatic. Go figure! However, by the time I completed primary school, this was sorted, and I also had a better grasp of the political system, its hows and whos. *Abelungu* came up tops for being instrumental in my suffering. Their bad attitude towards me and believing I was less than human – an ape – was etched into my child's mind. The law was 'their' law, and it definitely did not favour us as Africans. It is no mean thing to grow up understanding that you are not protected by the law, that in fact the law is your enemy.

As children, we said we did not believe *abelungu* were better than us, in other words, we were not inferior to them or anyone else. However, there was a truth we could not deny. The conditions of our living, the way we lived, how we lived, where we lived, all seemed to affirm our inferiority, including the food we ate – not from choice but because of affordability, or lack thereof. Our homes and where they were and how they looked, what they were made of as well as the impermanence of it all. The police daily hounded our parents. For the pass book. For liquor they were not permitted and liquor they sold and any number of other misdemeanours we children knew nothing about but the police did, and laws which the grownups daily flouted. In the blink of an eye, a family could be forced to leave – endorsed out of what the apartheid government termed the 'Designated Area of the Western Cape' and not allowed to return.

It did not help that the political system encouraged and supported white arrogance. As late as the mid-1980s, when racially insulted or attacked, most black people would let it go or pay it no overt attention – for the simple reason that this protected them from further insult or violence. This does not mean that the insult inflicted no wound. All black people are the Walking Internally-bleedings. The wounding is daily, ongoing. So is the bleeding. A white could call a black person the most hurtful name, and the court would find that white person not guilty – that is, if the black person had had the nerve, the time, the inclination and resources to lay charges. Most didn't, and the few who could often chose the less strenuous road.

Even in school, although we all knew it was illegal to do so, our teachers often referred to government policy or the unfairness of the political system; most of this was done indirectly but there were times the teacher would be so fed-up, so angry, an outburst would be scathing and direct: *Ezi zinja zamaBhulu!*[2] Needless to say, talking ill of *abelungu* did not feel bad. We did not see it as a bad thing to badmouth *abelungu* because they were so evil, they deserved to be referred to in as unflattering a manner as possible. In fact, could we ourselves do or say anything even remotely as evil as what they did and were doing to us? In short, we felt quite justified in any negative gesture or word directed at white people. It would not have occurred to us that what we did was anything other than simple racism.

Did we even realise we were imitating the people whose actions towards us we resented? Does hating someone who hates you heal you? Actually, we felt quite justified in our own little hate world because *abelungu* were the root cause of race hate. They hated us first. They thought and said bad things about us first. Did awful things to us first. Came to our land, found us happy in ourselves, then robbed us of everything. Why, then, would we have praised *abelungu*? Was I aware I was imbibing hate – race hate – and what the effects of this toxic mixture would be on my child self?

Claim #2: The most obvious manifestation of racialism occurs in the context of a power differential, where one group acts upon its racist theories by using violence to control another group of people. But racialism also occurs when one group of people thinks about, talks about, and collectively passes on disparaging ideas about another group. This more subtle brand of racialism is damaging in its own way; it creates a culture of continued racialism, discourages authentic interaction, and locks in notions of superiority and inferiority.

It is a well-known fact that no two people are identical. Strangely, though, in race theories, all those of same skin tone are 'classified' as one, a single group! When I think of the diversity within my own immediate family with its eight children, I would be lying if I said any two of us are alike in any manner or form. Yes, there are similarities here and there, between this one and that one. But then, these also exist between any two people anywhere – two totally unrelated people! That I have a certain talent or not, or like or dislike something – characteristics I may share with one or two or several of my siblings – proves absolutely nothing. I may – no, I do, as a matter of fact – share the same talents with certain people I know and others I do not know and will never know. That is life.

And then we 'classify' whole nations into homogenous 'groups': "'They" are such and such; lack this or that capability; will behave thus and not do blah!'

Growing up in apartheid South Africa, I was painfully aware of racial classification and that it entailed prejudice, especially against me. I did not understand the premise. I did not like it at all. In fact, I despised the conditions under which we lived even though, at first, I did not understand the why of it. Again, in an unstated way, I envied the white children for seeming to live a charmed life. They had everything any child could wish for; theirs seemed, to me, a dream life, a life made in heaven. Although my family was never the poorest in the locations we lived in, we were certainly not rich. None of the families around us were. Wealth was not for those classified 'Bantu' under apartheid. Indeed, any African man or woman who seemed to be doing well financially aroused the immediate suspicion of the authorities. And, most of the time, this was warranted. It was nigh impossible for an African to be wealthy after colonialism had firmly established itself.

A reasonable life could still be had in the rural areas where folk lived off the land. But the lure of money had gripped Africans by the tongue ... they had tasted what money got them and wanted more and more and more.

Even though our house in the Cape Town location had become a home away from home for new arrivals, we did not complain (children didn't do that then!); any new arrival was both welcome and resented by us children. Welcome for *umphako*[3] they brought with them – resented for the inconvenience that befell us children. The overcrowding meant we had to give up the privilege of our bed – among many other sacrifices. But, like most of our suffering, we put such inconveniences squarely on the shoulders of the apartheid government. The laws of *abelungu* made people poor. Forced husbands to leave their wives and children. We were aware of our exceedingly good fortune, having both parents in Cape Town, legally. So, what was a little inconvenience, now and then?

In my mid-twenties, I woke up to the fact that nothing in one's life can change without one's active participation in pursuing a goal. That led to my getting involved in organisations working for non-racialism in our country, and swiftly becoming an anti-apartheid spokesperson of some note. In January 1976, I was one of two South African delegates to the 'International Tribunal on Crimes Against Women', an event held in Brussels, Belgium. It was there that I awoke to the startling fact that racialism was not an exclusively South African phenomenon. A shock to my system was the realisation of the hypocrisy of the rest of the world. Yes, making racialism legal, part of the constitution, was going too far, but South African whites were doing what was being done all over the world. They had just legalised racialism, defended it using the Christianity brought to this part of the world by none other than themselves or their fathers and grandfathers.

I returned much energised by the support the work I was doing – with others, of course, never alone! – received from women in the Scandinavian countries, especially Norway and Sweden. I continued working for attitude change in women's groups, youth groups, church groups … sharing and growing … till I left South Africa in 1982 to study abroad. All this time, I did not regard myself as a racialist. Indeed, I was busy helping my country (white people, that is) rid itself of this nefarious characteristic, working for peaceful change. Racialists were white people – and, yes, some coloured people and almost all Asiatics. Not a few leading anti-apartheid activists – lawyers, doctors, etc. – were thus classified ('Asiatic' and 'coloured'), but this did not stop 'Bantus' believing that those 'groups' were racialist too, just as whites were.

While studying at Columbia University in New York, I got a part-time job at the United Nations and later joined the institution as a full-time staff member. It was early in this period of my life, working and living in New York, that I met the late Peggy Dye. Peggy and I loved reading. We also loved talking, sharing ideas and exchanging news and views, especially from books we were reading. During one of those sessions, Peggy introduced me to the book *Exterminate All the Brutes*, a searing exposé by Sven Lindqvist.[4] A whole deep hole of horror opened. I began to understand the deep-rooted nature of race hate; an evil based on the research early scientists had conducted in Africa and whose intellectual exertions were awarded doctoral degrees by universities such as Cambridge and Oxford. Oh, and loads of money, too – from the British Crown, among other benefactors and supporters of 'progress'. Their breathtakingly bigoted work – a feather in the cap for the British Empire – was spectacularly applauded and books were written based on the findings of these 'scientists'.

Strangely, at first, the book left me absolutely flabbergasted; this was the first time I had read anything like it, or that specific, which spelled out the early history of racialism. Then I asked: how could anyone write down, in black and white, such a horrible account of this thing? How could any publisher publish this disgrace? As if *not* writing about it would mean it had not happened. But when has hiding anything ever lessened its impact? Yes, I had glimpsed the depth of race hate and better understood its effects. The nameless 'thing' I carried in my heart and mind as a result of race hate was not just racialism – the word, idea or phenomenon – but what it meant, had meant and, more painfully, what it had done, to me as a person. The dreadful 'othering' and 'insult' and deprivation and oppression it had piled on my head, implanted in my soul. For the white-skinned person, there is no easy way to escape their fate: the superiority complex is deep-seated in the very soul of white people. The only difference is how individuals, born white-skinned, use what history claims for them, and the privileges it bestows on them. Is there a questioning? An understanding? A response, or simple acceptance … this last, understandable, for it is convenient. Yes, for whites, racialism is a convenient – enriching – privilege.

Overt racialism has, and rightly so, been broadly condemned. Even in South Africa, ever since the late 1980s, before the official end of apartheid with the first truly democratic elections in 1994, racialism had begun to lose its legal status. However, that fact does not mean it is no longer overt. Here and there, now and again, in our beautiful South Africa, it still rears its ugly, monstrous head. We read headlines of white university students peeing on a sleeping black student or on a black person's belongings; people are turned away from a restaurant or a shop, warning us all that overt racism has not died. We live with daily notices and reminders of that ugly wound in the soul of South Africa.

And what about subtle racialism? How is it perceived?

When I finally came to the startling, awful realisation that I was not only a racist but also racialistic in the beliefs I held – most of which were held unconsciously – I soon saw that I needed to be both honest and ruthless with myself. Vigilance is nothing if, when you catch yourself in the act, you lie to yourself, pretend what happened did not happen or, worse still, was warranted.

I had been involved in anti-apartheid activism, working for peaceful change in South Africa, working mostly on attitude change. Now there's a laugh! I believed the attitudes that needed changing were those of white people. Whites were the problem. Whites harboured negative stereotypes about us black people. Why didn't I see that, by lumping all whites together, I was doing exactly what I was condemning white people for doing: judging a group of people by the colour of their skin? The imbecility of it! Perpetrating the very 'crime' you accuse another of committing – and directing your bigoted act at the accused!

Where does the black-skinned person fit into this scheme? Denial or acceptance? Outrage too, of course. Anecdotally, most black people do not believe they are racialists, that is, not liking white people or mixed-race or Indian people. And if you challenge them, all to quickly comes the refrain: 'Well, look how they treat us! How they look down on us! How they think they are better than us!' Though of course, when you point an accusing finger at someone, four point back at you! However, our learnt behaviour is so deep-seated that it is nigh impossible to not consider skin colour in our interactions with others. Yes, most people will say skin colour shouldn't matter – but it *does* matter.

Any time we change our behaviour, including verbal behaviour, because the person with whom we are interacting is of a different skin colour, that is racialism. We all have to learn anew that people are the same, irrespective of skin colour. Therefore, we should treat them the same, which is not so difficult to figure out. The old saying: 'Do unto others as you would have them do unto you' is an excellent guide. This would minimise the risk of 'othering' people with whom we interact – at work, at places of worship, in school, in a shop or just walking down the road. Wherever people encounter one another, there should be the expectation of civility, whether they speak the same tongue or not, wear the same colour skin or not.

Claim #3: The imputation of inferiority is hard to shake off. But rather than spending energy trying to identify and shame individuals who are presumed to be 'racist', we should be investing in the critical work that is needed to overcome the lingering effects of centuries of systematised racialism.

Feeling inferior came fairly naturally to me. The second born, coming after a male child. As if that were not grief enough, I was an ugly baby, while my brother was a Greek god – a situation that did not change in my teens and beyond. Then, I am small in stature (though I prefer petite to short!). That tells you how I feel about my physical self. And where I did excel, in school, others threw these shortcomings back at me, as if in retaliation. It didn't help that I was always one of the youngest in my class. Or that I was a bit of a braggart. And so, feeling inferior to the perceived superiority of white children and white people (in short, the white world) seemed normal.

The world of work didn't help much either. I stumbled along as best I could … now and then getting into arguments over perceived slights, mostly at shops, where I felt my money was as good as any white person's, demanding civility from those who served me. However, as I grew older and my situation slowly changed for the better, I began to believe I had mastered the art of carrying myself in ways that disguised my feelings of inadequacy.

But can I lay my hands on the Bible and say that I've overcome the inferiority complex that has been as constant as a shadow to me – constant and inescapable? Not really. Feelings of inadequacy leap into my body, freezing it numb. Self-doubt persists, for memory is tenacious. Whether shopping or in conversation or accidentally bumping into someone at a gathering, stranger or not, meeting in that context – all it takes is a word, a look or some facial expression, often furtive, or a silence in the conversation, a silence that shouts louder than the roar of thunder, disrupting the conversation mid-word, or a word repeated, and … ZI-III-NNG/POING!

> A flash bright and bitter
> At once springs into my mind
> Been there
> Done that
> Same, same old story.
> Will I ever measure up?
> Will I?
> When you made up your white
> Mind I didn't
>
> Couldn't
> Never would
> All those centuries ago … and
>
> You never will
>
> Can't
> Never did
> Let go of the lie
> Grand antecedent
> Sealed any crack in
> Your blind
> Soul.

While the belief in the superiority of white skin over black skin is what usually dominates discussions of race, my poem suggests I am also concerned with the inverse of that phenomenon – that is, the perceived inferiority of black skin to white skin in the minds of black skin people. The two exist and work together to maintain the fallacy. Shall we call the phenomenon 'black complicity'?

Proof of this is seen in the way that black people who are aware of racial dynamics are forever, painstakingly careful to not 'confirm' stereotypes whites might hold of the black group. Make sure nothing goes 'missing' – leave no trace of my having been in your house or toilet, not even at work, as that would confirm what you already believe about me – that I am a filthy being incapable of automatic neatness as you whites are; eat carefully, slowly, when in your company, and make sure to consume less than I ordinarily would (don't be greedy); get embarrassed when other blacks do not seem aware they are 'on trial' and behave as though they were back in the hood; things such as loud noises deep into the night, or rowdy behaviour during the day, too much make up or accessories, etc., etc., ad infinitum.

Respectable, highly educated, world-renowned academics suffer the same apprehensiveness when they cross over to the world of white privilege where they know and have experienced prejudice. Should we go to this hotel or restaurant? Will we be treated 'normally' or with the usual suspicious, furtive glances and codes, and assumptions like 'Here we go, again! Watch! "They" can't afford anything here', being shown to some crappy corner near the kitchen so as not to offend better prospects who, on catching sight of our blackness, will turn around and leave?

That such thoughts are the norm for black people, not only in South Africa but elsewhere too, indicates that although they may not actually believe in their inferiority, the mere knowledge of its universal existence in the white world cannot but bother them, hound them, hurt them … every single day of their waking lives.

Belief systems can lead to action, which in turn leads to the implanting of ideas based on those beliefs, embedding them in the minds of those who suffer the consequences of the actions. Where, on first encounter, neutrality may have prevailed, subsequent interaction, influenced by a race-based belief system, means that those with eyes to see and ears to hear cannot escape the negative indoctrination that flows from the system.

Today, no black person will openly admit to feeling inferior to white people; however, the actions of most proclaim it out loud. Thus, in jest, someone might chastise or tease another for appearing superior in some way, and say, 'Don't go all white on me!' In manner of dress, in speech, complexion, hairstyle – especially women and girls – the closer to 'whiteness' one gets, the better; that, at any rate, is the underlying assumption, which is seldom verbalised or acknowledged. But the vigilant will ask themselves: 'better?' – says who?

Better, because it is in fact better, or simply because it approximates 'whiteness'?

Not that there is anything wrong with enjoying what one enjoys, but one must be aware of choices one makes, and what those are based upon. We must call ourselves out when we find ourselves 'whiting ourselves' – *sizenza abelungu*[5] – and ask ourselves whose standards we are applying and what benefit this brings us as black people.

But perhaps the worst sign of the hurt is in the deep-seated, soul-fouling, heart-numbing littleness in all black people. No ambition, some would say. No aspirations others might say. But who can dare dream when, implanted in her genetic makeup is a negative of the doctoral-awarded geniuses of centuries ago and the indoctrination this birthed, implanted and reinforced over and over again as the 'civilised' went about infesting the entire world with their supremacy in terms of belief systems, warfare, commercial aptitude. To this day, native races suffer the consequences and are aware that they suffer, that they are oppressed – they are regarded as 'less than'. What does this do to the psyche of people thus subjected to systemic racialism? It cannot but bruise their psyche, brutalise their soul. This has resulted in the targeted antagonism in black-to-white actions such as murders. For there are cases where robbery is clearly not the motive for a killing, but rather revenge: black anger-driven revenge for historical hurts.

What will it take to be free of these reactions, to transcend the deep-seated alienation that results in personal harms in the name of race? Something that helped me recently in thinking about this question was the work by American professor Robin DiAngelo on white fragility[6] and the defence mechanisms white people employ when experiencing racial tension. It sent me down memory lane – to when I had first read Lindqvist's *Exterminate All the Brutes*. I have revisited it over and over again, and done so voluntarily too, even though the book had shocked me on first encounter and subsequently filled me with anger each time; anger I carry to this day, although I believe I have mastered it and used it to my benefit and, hopefully, that of others who are seeking escape from the scourge of racialism. Listening in on a broadcast interview with DiAngelo as she spoke about white fragility, I again experienced shock but, bit by reluctant bit, I slowly came to a complete conversion. The learned professor made sense. Pure and simple. She explained the simplicity and totality of the 'racism' (or racialism in my terms) that confounds us all.

However, in her work she addresses only the 'racism' of white people. That left me wondering: as a black person, I have for a long time seen this racialism as a one-way street – white people to black people – but what is to be said about the other street? White people 'invented' race hate with the silly excuse of doing 'research' centuries ago. Deep-seated as the resultant myth of white supremacy is in whitehood, it has long been determined to be a falsehood of epic proportions. However, there can be no denying that race hate impacts black lives negatively and continuously, relentlessly. What is a black body to do? Thinking about it subsequent to my encounter with DiAngelo, I came up with the following guidelines for myself, and, if asked, I would 'offer' them to black people – despite the fact that I do not subscribe to group mentality, or 'groupthink':

Know and accept the inescapable perception of your 'inferiority'. This does not mean that you *are* inferior. Accepting the existence of this perception of whites does not mean you must believe what the white person believes about you. Just know the fact that whites (those who have not deliberately distanced themselves from mainstream ideas) see you as not only differently coloured but differently abled and inferior to how nature endowed them – not only mentally, but also in terms of your capacity to grow and develop in other ways. Know that fact, and know what you need to do. It is not your job to teach that white person you are not inferior. Your job is to know the lie that exists in the heart and in the soul of the unaware white person. Know that lie, and live your life with the full knowledge that the white person is carrying that burden in their soul, and it determines interactions they have with you; this sad fact cannot but be so.

Your job is believing in *ubuntu bakho* – your inherent humanity. Nothing anyone does or says or believes or writes or decrees can diminish that. Living with and in that belief carries the obligation to *live morally*. Live a life that harms none – whether human or non-human, animate or non-animate – in other words, live and let live!

White racialism should not force black you into black racialism. Then you yourself are a racialist. If white racialism is a scourge, so is black racialism, and neither is excusable. But they are fact. Racialism is fact. White racialism; black racialism – both are fact. Sad fact!

Our challenge, as black people, is to determine what to do. How to live unsullied in the face of this inescapable toxic racialistic labelling that we know is at all times and in all circumstances levelled against us. Consciously, mostly, but sometimes unconsciously. For it is always there.

Live with the knowledge of what racialism means and will mean all your life. Be aware of it and take a stand that says you do not support racialism. That means you live your life in full knowledge of its being, to a not small degree, the outcome of inescapable ideology. That is conscientious awareness. Ask yourself the hard questions when the situation calls for it. Why am I reacting in this way? Is it because the person provoking me is white? Is the action or the skin colour the trigger? Would I react in the same way were the person before me of the same skin colour as I am? Am I using skin colour, allowing it to determine my action, reaction or inaction?

My personal cross, what irritates me most – and frequently – is when someone who is not African calls me 'mama' when I know, and they know, if they are honest with themselves, that they would not call me that were I not 'Bantu', that is, black black. On the other hand, I suppose I should be grateful; mama is an upgrade from what we black black women were called in the not-too-distant past: 'Jane' – the generic name by which an adult black woman was generally addressed by white men, women and children. And those whites who 'Janed' black women in this way, stripping us of our identity and individuality, professed being unable to pronounce our 'difficult' names with their 'clicks'. Si-ndi-we – see any clicks in that name? Do not forget either, that these were the kinder whites. There were those who called us 'K...'.[7] These days, when anyone calls me 'mama' when I know they know nothing about my culture apart from this one exception that racialism has popularised, I'm apt to challenge them, if only by ignoring them, not responding to their greeting or whatever. However, I have on occasion reacted in a fiery way – much to the surprise of the person who'd addressed me 'politely' as their 'mama' or 'Jane'.

I have commanded myself thus: Be brutally honest with yourself.

Absolve yourself from guilt. You did not manufacture racialism. You were not born with it. It was taught to you – you have learnt it – whether consciously or unconsciously. Willingly, actively or otherwise. The truth is that you have not escaped inhaling it. No one can; it is in the very air we breathe as humans.

Black complicity in racialism centres on anger – burning anger directed at white racialism, which is omnipresent and daily grinds black you down to the very marrow in your bones. Anger and blame make a victim of you, and victimhood is never empowering. Indeed, the victimhood that race-hate breeds results in disempowerment – to the extent that black reaction to the deep-seated hurt does little to alleviate that hurt. Nor does it cure – or indeed hurt – those who had originally inflicted that hurt. An example of this might be spectators rejoicing at white defeat on the sports field: 'Yaa, they were beaten! They're not as mighty as they think they are!' But how does that elevate your own status as a black person? Even in your own eyes, how does this elevate you? Does it alleviate any of your suffering?

To my fellow humans: knowing and accepting that you are, and cannot be other than, racist or racialist, it is up to you to monitor your racialism, weed out what you find abhorrent. Be forever vigilant – towards yourself, your family, your friends, and others in your circle. You and I are the keepers of those whose company we keep. Acknowledge and accept the inescapability of racialism. Stop as much of the rot as you can, try to eliminate it, and do not judge others. Be aware of the poison you carry; mind you never use it.

The present generation of adults, particularly those like me of advanced age, bear a particularly onerous responsibility regarding the passing on of racialism. Let us do all we can, all in our power, to stop the evil that has for so long ruined what would have been a heaven on earth. Each one of us should undertake the task of consciously and conscientiously disrupting racialism. Do not pass on what was passed onto you by your forebears. It is up to you. It is up to me. Together, we can thin the spread, we can stop the flow, of this specific poison by not passing it on to those we nurture, those who depend on us to become fully human. Help them to grow up unstained by racialism.

To reiterate, we are all born without any knowing, including that of different skin colour. We learn this as soon as we encounter it, and there is no avoiding that, for skin colour is a visible difference, everywhere around us, as it is part of humanity. However, we soon learn the attitudes, mostly negative, linked to skin colour from our parents, families, friends, relatives, teachers, neighbours, religious organisations, newspapers – in short, negative attitudes about those of a different skin colour abound. A child, even one raised by parents who are themselves not overtly racialistic, cannot escape picking this up from the environment – it is inescapable. Everyone sees colour. However, some believe skin colour determines ability and character – that is racialism, and can be corrected; indeed, it should and must be corrected. We are all racists, but we are not all racialists, and nor should we be, for that is a choice we make and, if we find ourselves already 'infected' we can and should take remedial action.

Therefore, if one is determined to not be a racialist, one has to first acknowledge the inescapable fact of already being that – whether it is intentional, whether acquired consciously or not; one has to admit the sad (and painful/ugly) fact to oneself upon becoming aware, waking up to the fact, that this is what one is: a racialist. And that is what I myself had to do … eventually. But why, you may ask, should racialism be dispensed with? The answer is simple: because doing so is the right thing to do – it is the *human* thing to do. Anything that works against nature is wrong – evil, even. Human beings, all human beings, are part of nature – like the grass and the trees, the mountains and rivers and seas. Hurting any of these is not only wrong but disturbs and could even destroy life itself. Human beings are not of greater worth than plants or animals. Indeed, the upsurge of the Green Movement, the awareness of the earth's vulnerability, should give us pause. We should ask ourselves, 'What about the damage we inflict on one another?' It is not my intention to weigh one misdeed against another – but racialism kills the core of the victim's personhood. Right now, I weep for multi-coloured humanity – hopefully, however, soon my tears will no longer need to flow.

PART III
WRITING ABOUT MY WRITING

This section features essays in which Sindiwe Magona reflects upon the most significant and best-known works in her oeuvre. Two of the pieces were previously published while four represent new writing. In their discussion of the origins, the process, and, in some cases, the reception of each text, they serve as enlightening supplements to her literary works. But they are so rich with unique and engaging reflections on a wide variety of social issues that each stands independent of its corresponding work. When these 'Why I Wrote' essays are considered together, they provide a window into Magona's thoughts over the years and across her different creative productions, and also into Magona's expanding sense of herself as a writer.

9.

WHY I WROTE MY AUTOBIOGRAPHIES

This essay, which was published in Five Points: A Journal of Literature and Art *in Winter 2018, was originally titled 'The Impact of Colonialism & Post-colonialism on Women's Writing'. In it, Sindiwe Magona explains her first encounter with writing and how she stumbled upon autobiography, and reflects upon the significance of life writing in her own development as a writer.*

AT A CONFERENCE I once attended, a writer (white) made the startling (to me, at any rate) assertion that Cecil Rhodes brought apples to South Africa. This came after some of us (African writers) had been going on, decrying colonialism and the hardships and disruption it had brought to the African continent. I suppose she was putting us in our place or, as the saying goes, setting the record straight.

I bring this up because it is also true that colonialism brought writing to South Africa. It also brought us the English language. However, because the nature of colonialism was never one of equality between the colonisers and the colonised, the inequality affected all aspects of life and living, including writing.

The English language and writing was in most probability taught to natives with the view of serving the coloniser and his purpose, which may broadly be described as trade and spreading Christianity.

I was born into a Christian family and went to a mission school for my primary school education. Even when I was at high school, even though it was not a church school, the day started with assembly, where we had hymn-singing and prayers, usually in English. At home, I do not recall much attention being paid to the language of the child, except for the first burst of happy surprise when the baby starts making sounds that announce she is attempting human speech. Oh, yes, then there is much encouragement. However, that soon stops as the baby becomes a toddler and then a child and her speech is taken for granted. It is at school that I recall receiving praise for my use of language. However, although that praise was for both spoken and written language, not one of my teachers, right up to teacher-training college, ever hinted that there might be a writer hidden somewhere inside me. The idea of developing a skill, in which I showed clear promise, was simply never imparted to me. This is no surprise, given the political situation in the country at that time. Journalism was the purview of white men and women, thanks to legislation providing for job reservation.[1]

People do as other people do – we call that role modelling. I was almost thirty years old before I held a book in my hand that had been written by someone who looked vaguely like me – Maya Angelou, an African-American woman. One can safely make the assumption that it had never occurred to me I might write a book, never mind understand the whole business of writing – that is, that writing can be a career! Dreams are like madness, and they are culture-based. One is only able to dream of that which one has actually seen, just as one's hallucinations are bound and determined by one's cultural background. We don't all 'see' the same bizarre things when we go outside of reality.

The colonising people dominate the people they colonise. Embedded in that is the assumed superiority of the coloniser's culture. One of the cruellest outcomes is that the colonised eventually 'accept' the inferior status imposed on them. This is not to say they like it, but colonialism would not have gone on as long as it did in Africa (and elsewhere) had there been no collusion – overt or covert – on the part of the colonised.

That I did not know or dream I could write is part of that acceptance of inferiority. White people wrote books; I was not white. All the books of my early childhood (not that there were many!) were written by white people, even those in my mother tongue, isiXhosa. Later on, the names of African men appeared on the covers of a few readers, but most times, these were in the company of the names of white men. Immediately, I understood that the African men were helping a little – here and there, perhaps translating an obscure word the big white master had not met before. But the white men were doing the actual writing.

I may have been wrong in that assumption, but all evidence pointed to that fact: the school inspectors were all white men. (It has occurred to me, as I write, that I never met a female school inspector – never questioning this – never mind a black female school inspector!)

Then, Africa woke up; its people wanted to rid the continent of the colonisers. The unthinkable happened when Ghana became independent. Soon thereafter, country after country shed the yolk of colonialism. Then burst forth African literature and although in apartheid South Africa most of this excitement remained out of reach for us, there were instances when excellence simply could not be kept out. This happened, for instance, with Chinua Achebe's *Things Fall Apart*, which was prescribed for Matric English (for white schools!). Sadly, there are still millions of us black Africans who have not read a single book by this remarkable writer, or by any other of the numerous illustrious African writers! Writers from other places (South America, the East – middle, near, and far) are, for the majority of us, still uncharted territory.

In the meantime, though, the debate about the evils of colonialism and apartheid in South Africa was heating up, and I had become part of it. It was engagement in anti-apartheid work, inside the country, working for what we called 'peaceful change', that opened my eyes to the startling fact that most white people did not have a clue about what it meant to be me. They had no idea what it meant to live under the harsh, irksome, constant restraints imposed by apartheid laws.

Now, don't get me wrong, I am no apologist for white South Africa, whose policy inflicted apartheid on the rest of us. But, believe it or not, I had bought into the lie of white superiority. No, I did not 'accept' it, though unconsciously I must have believed it. Something – call it the environment – must have poured this lie into my heart and mind. I thought, and knew, that all white people know it all, are naturally brilliant, etc. Imagine my surprise, then, to come to the realisation that most had little understanding of the impact of their policies. That is not the same as saying they should not have made it their business to know what it was they were doing – what running the country for their exclusive benefit meant for the rest of us. They made the laws that governed us all, while we had no say in the making of those laws, nor in the appointment of those who made them.

But things were a-changing. It was the attitude-change work we did, the speeches, meetings, workshops, encounter groups that made me aware not only of the lack of knowledge about each other as people of South Africa, but also the surprising ordinariness of people, irrespective of skin colour!

Feelings often ran high at encounters between the races. But it was from these encounters that I learnt to value my own truth – what I knew, what I believed in, and who I was. What astounded me, perhaps confounded would be a better word, was that these were the people who wrote books, including history books. All the history books I had ever come across, certainly those used in our schools during my time, were written by white men.

More and more, it became clearer that we owe it to our children's children – those who will people this land long after we are gone – to leave footprints, to say in our own words what it was to be the people we were: subjugated, despised and deprived of the most basic of human rights. I am convinced they will be more than eager or curious to hear from us, in fact eager to hear what it was like living under apartheid, what it was to live without the benefit of citizenship in the country of one's birth; to live as a slave, without being called one. This, they should hear from our own lips – the words we leave for them, words from our pens. It shouldn't be that even our suffering is reported only by those who inflicted that suffering on us. This was a huge debate in the not-so-distant past: Why do white people write about us? I subscribed to the debate until it dawned on me that a white man or woman writing about me does not stop *me* from writing about me. Of course, when the thought finally came to me, it didn't come dragging the requisite writing skills with it! I did not have the vaguest idea of how to write or what to write – never mind the rest.

But the worst of it was the gnawing fear that the realisation brought. Who did I think I was? Who would publish a book written by me? And where would I start writing that book?

Feelings of inferiority birth untold insecurity. If I woke up, in my late twenties, to the realisation that I should write, it took me another two decades to act on that realisation. It is a hard, hard task to chip away at a lifetime belief.

Thus it is that I came to writing rather late in life – in my late forties. Suddenly, it became urgent, imperative, that I tell the story of South Africa: apartheid South Africa. I now saw clearly that when I died, my truth died. What I knew, felt, loved and cherished – what I detested, feared, or desired most … all these things would be no more, just as I would be no more. It didn't matter how vital they were; unless there was some record of them, they would disappear. Now, I became even more scared of my failure to write than the ridicule I was certain I risked in actually writing.

Blindly, if with a sense of urgency, I began writing. Yes, I still knew I knew nothing about writing, but I'd also discovered that not everybody knew everything, and, what is more important: there were things I knew I knew, knew for sure; and had come to know that those things – some very, very important things, crucial in my life and in lives such as mine – were absolutely beyond the ken of others. Now, this was a void I wished to disrupt. If we were ever to reconcile as the people of this country, getting to know who we were, know and appreciate and respect our diversity, introducing one another to our who-ness, our *ubuni bethu*, our essence, would have to be a first step. Biographies – including autobiographies, I surmised – were best suited to this endeavour, in my humble opinion.

Coming to writing with limitations I was painfully aware of, I wrote about what I knew best, knew without the shadow of a doubt: my life. Not being schooled in the art, I fell back onto the storytelling tradition of my long-ago childhood. And, thus began what ended up as two books of autobiography, although that was not the intended outcome. I ended up writing the story of my life after a lot of hesitation, painful questions, and frightful starts and stops. I tried to write just about everything before I resorted to autobiography. However, each thing I wrote – be it short story, novel, or drama – showed signs that, to me, said those details came from my life. Some high-school teacher had once told me: 'Fiction is something that never happened'. Take it from me, anyone who attempts to write a book about something that never happened, that is a book that will likely never happen. I know. I tried to do just that.

So, one would be justified in saying I turned to autobiography with some measure of desperation. I told myself that, since every piece of writing I attempted tended to be a little about me, I would go ahead and write about me. The reasoning was that I believed I would clear that part of my brain that controls creativity. Clear it of me and everything about me. Since I also knew that nature does not allow a vacuum, it stood to reason, I thought, that something 'not about me' would then come to occupy that space vacated by 'all about me'; that is what I would then proceed to write about.

I had no sooner found a way out of my quandary than I encountered another. 'Who the hell would want to read about your life?' whispered a small but strident voice, deep inside the well of my being. Really, whatever had happened in my so painfully ordinary life that I should imagine anyone would be interested in it, never mind be so interested that they would go and buy a book and then read it … a book all about Sindiwe Magona. Ordinary Sindiwe Magona!

Then, in what I've heard Oprah Winfrey call 'a lightbulb moment', the great métier, archaeology, came to my rescue. Does that make me a fossil?

Jokes aside, it was recalling the work of excavators that freed me from the fear of my insipid life and made it into a jewel worth preserving. However, this did not make me so bold that I anticipated being read by present-day readers. Oh, no! My book, the story of my life, would shed light on an ordinary person's life during the dark ages of our country. Generations to come, wondering what, exactly, apartheid meant, would read my book and be enlightened.

I am a history major. I knew that nothing lasts forever, civilisations come and go, even the greatest have crumbled over time. Why, then, would apartheid last for ever?

No, I didn't foresee that apartheid would die while I was still alive, no one did. Not in South Africa or anywhere else in the world. That evil system appeared so entrenched, so formidable, we prayed future generations might be spared but hardly hoped the same for ourselves. It just didn't seem possible.

Well, thus freed from what I perceived as the embarrassing reality of my life, I put pen to paper, holding nothing back. Today, I get complimented on the frankness of my autobiography. What people do not realise is, I was that frank because I did not imagine I would be confronted by readers of the book of the story of my life. That had not occurred to me. I was writing for posterity. The title of the first part, *To My Children's Children* (1990), refers not to my biological offspring but the people who will live long after I am no more. I doubt I would ever have revealed everything I did, or done so with such frankness if I had known, could have foreseen, living people with whom I might come into contact reading what I wrote. Timidity is another of the crippling legacies of apartheid. Timidity and a sense of shame … even about things that were not of our doing. Why have I spent my adult life – a great deal of it, at any rate, ashamed that I grew up in a shack?

To My Children's Children

However, that shame is something that grew as I grew into the writing. When I was living these experiences, I was not at all ashamed. How is a baby to feel ashamed because she is born in a mud hut, a rondavel? What toddler is shamed by a shortage of napkins or nutritious food? If more than half the class doesn't have books, the parents too poor to afford the purchase, why would you be ashamed you are one of that crowd? My childhood was a typical childhood for a child of people the apartheid government labelled 'Bantu' and barred from each and every civil opportunity, things most of the world take for granted, givens in modern living. I narrated that reality without any sense of shame for, as already mentioned, I was writing for future people. Naturally, that called for absolute honesty, candour – this was history, if only on a personal level. I was sure my manuscript would be invaluable to those in the far-distant future, social scientists of various kinds, who were looking back, researching our Now, their Then. In pursuit of such clarity, I painstakingly wrote down every detail, event or episode that I could recall, things that made up the life I had led, from birth, right up to the moment I had written *To My Children's Children*. I was, at that point, nearer forty than thirty.

But the publisher, though delighted to have the book, was against publishing such a voluminous one by 'an unknown writer'. I was entering a whole new world – the world of book publishing.

After Marie Philip, editor as well as the other half and full partner of David Philip Publishers, had painstakingly explained the whole enchilada and I had begun to glimpse some advantage in the suggested arrangement (another book!), I took on the challenge. I am not saying I leapt for joy. However, after further explanation, I also saw that I did not have to write a whole new book, but simply rework the beginning and end of the section that was cut. Having just written the book – first in long hand and then having typed the whole thing after learning to use a typewriter – I had some inkling that this was not going to be a walk in the park, though.

The rearrangement involved ending one book and starting the sequel. Not much emboldened by having my manuscript accepted, I quivered at the prospect of being discovered/unveiled as a sham of a writer. What if I could not do this? Could not convincingly wrap up the one book, part one of my autobiography, and begin the sequel, part two?

Writing, I was coming to see, was about just doing it. You may not get it right at once – but try, try, and try again. I was lucky with splitting the manuscript into two, for I found a happy division between the two: happy, not emotionally, but an event that worked for the writing – the end of my first marriage. Although we were not divorced, my husband had left Cape Town – without consultation or even mention of his intention. I could not go to Johannesburg, where he subsequently resurfaced. Both of us would be in that area illegally. What was even more scary for me was that the move would jeopardise my 'qualification' to 'reside and work' in the prescribed area of the Western Cape – in accordance with Article 10 Section 1-B of one of the notorious Pass Laws. He, a migrant labourer, had nothing to lose or gain in either area. He qualified for residence in neither province. However, he could be (as he'd been when we met in the WC) permitted to be in any urban area as a migrant worker. As we were no longer in love, I realised that my staying put in the Western Cape, where he'd been permitted to work and where he had abandoned me, was for the better. Only decades later did I discover that this permission had been withdrawn and he was endorsed out of the area, for good.

The compelling story was in the detail. I, of course, didn't know that then. However, forced to write that 'ending', made me revisit what I had written as a summary. Now, I went into a little more detail, painted the how and when of it all. I had a given number of pages to fill and went about doing just that and found, to my absolute surprise and joy, that the more I told, the better the story sounded – even to me! The last two chapters of *To My Children's Children* – 'A Hard Finishing School' and 'Forced to Grow' – were the result of the outpouring of my story, with details I had not included, not told, not revealed in the original manuscript; not because I was being coy but through sheer inexperience or ineptitude. I had touched on my experiences as a domestic worker and my husband's miserliness. But now, he was gone and had done me the huge favour of 'losing' my job for me. I resorted to selling sheep heads – getting this cheap local food on credit from a respectable butcher. He was someone I held in high esteem. That I was forced to approach him and ask for credit, ask him to trust me, shows how desperate I was. I went to town telling him about my plans for the preparation, cooking and selling of the fare. There were hazards in this kind of business, giving credit to people who often found it difficult to meet their obligations. But there were those who took the risk, like this kindly man. The businesswoman I was forced to become discovered all this by trial and error, through experience. The plight of my children, their future, was uppermost in my mind and heart and propelled me forward. I had been given a chance at a better life, by two people who had never had that – my parents. I had some education. How could I live with myself if I failed not only to give my children as much as I had been given by my parents, but more – much more? Isn't that what is called progress? Each generation enabling the next to march but a step further on the road that is life? It had been a grave error, having children (and so many) at such an early age; having them without the necessary preparation or prerequisites. Now, a single parent, I was truly forced to grow so they themselves might become – realising their potential.

Forced to Grow

Fortuitously, *Forced to Grow* (1992) became the title of the sequel, whose preface indicates: 'Continuing the story of *To My Children's Children* ...'.

Nothing in my growing up had prepared me for single parenthood. By the tender age of 23, I had not only been dumped by my husband, I'd also lost my job as a domestic worker. I had grown up in poverty, but now I was plunged into destitution. However, I'd had the good fortune of parents who had taken their role as a God-given duty; they were good role models. I vowed to do the best I could to minimise the impact of their father's abandonment on my three children.

Not for me *ixhwele*[2] and his love potions to bring back an errant man. What energy I had, I saw clearly, I had to spend on improving myself, the only person I controlled. My destiny, and that of my children, was in my hands. No one was going to die and leave me a fortune, any improvement to our situation could only come through education. Belatedly, I remembered Mama's words of wisdom to her daughters: education is the only husband who will never leave you!

Certain I wanted nothing to do with men and the loving they purportedly offered (look where that had landed me!), I had also woken up to my own instability or fragility so far as that was concerned. The last thing I wanted or needed was another surprise pregnancy. I had already had the three that were now a burden on my shoulders – and my shoulders only. I would never, ever trust a man to do the right thing ... as Tata had done ... as I was brought up to believe all men did.

Fortunately, for me, the doctor attending me on my very first post-natal visit saw to that. Racism, I believe, underlay his offer. He matter-of-factly asked me, while at the same time advising against it: 'Do you and your husband want any more children? It is not safe to have more than three Caesarean sections, mama.'

I shook my head; not bothering to explain that there was no longer any husband in my life.

'Fine', said the doctor. He reached out for the trolley at his side, snatched a pad and, offering me a pen while he held it, said, 'Sign here', pointing to the blank space above a dotted line.

I felt he was acting out his racism. Yet I was one up on him. I wanted that outcome.

That taken care of, I was more than ready to venture into the future I wanted – the future I was busy planning. Second chances. Thus began my education, by correspondence, since the government of the day had closed all technical colleges that had been open to us. Matric; A-Levels (through London University, no less); Bachelor of Arts and, finally, a Master of Science degree from Columbia University – all apart from the last done by candlelight. These studies began while I was working as a domestic worker, and selling sheep heads and vetkoek to make invisible, never-there ends meet. In my desperation, I even attempted, once, to 'get rich quick' by getting hold of a bag of dagga. Deposited at my house on a Monday, if memory serves, I could not wait for the man to come 'collect' on Friday. That was one miserable week for a very, very scared me. I could smell jail. I expected to be arrested any minute. A week has a lot of anxiety-filled minutes. I gave him the unopened bag. He took one look, smiled, and left with his 'goods'. For, tempted though I was, I never sold any dagga to a single soul. Fear. And a sense of shame. Shame, I had even stooped to considering selling weed.

Today, I look back and know that what I saw then as misfortune was an opportunity. I am grateful to my God of Hope, to my parents (may they rest in peace) and to the many, many people (and organisations) who came to my assistance along the way.

Life is a gift. Mine was rescued from utter ruin when my situation became so desperate that I was forced to grow.

But how was I to start the sequel? I had ended the preceding book, *To My Children's Children*, on an upbeat note. Yes, the father of my children was gone, but I had started gathering myself together, or, at least, had made the decision to do that. It made sense therefore, to begin *Forced to Grow* at the same spot. Of course, I would not use the same words, but convey the sense of where I was, at what point in the life I was portraying in this book, this sequel to the other. Also, try to link the two in some way. Isn't life itself continuous, after all?

At this point, I was surprised by an uncharacteristically far-from-shy me coming out through the narration of this part of my life story. For I was able to acknowledge the hard truths of that period of my life, acknowledge these without feeling worthless.

Yes, I was already a 'has-been', my life finished, at the age of twenty-three. Sans husband, I was the mother of two little girls and expecting my third child – as it turned out, a son. He was born in October 1966, four months after his father had left us.

Looking back, I can see how I managed to write what I wrote, to say it out like that. For, by the time I was writing my life story, I had long left that space of being a 'has-been'. An employee of the United Nations Organization, working at headquarters in New York, I had already shed a lot of the disempowering sense of shame that apartheid-made poverty had planted in my very soul. Not altogether shame-free … but the journey had begun. That is one of the benefits of writing, especially writing one's life story. It gives the writer another perspective on a life she thought she knew intimately. In other words, autobiographical writing can lead to self-revelation and self-discovery. It certainly did, for me.

While 'telling' the story of the road I had travelled, from destitution in apartheid South Africa to working for Anti-Apartheid Radio, a section of United Nations Radio, itself part of the UN Department of Public Information, the realisation hit me: 'She could do it too!' – and the face of someone I knew, someone in South Africa who was in the dire straits I had been in my early twenties, would come up right before my eyes. Trouble is, I also knew she was no isolated case. There were millions and millions of these 'has beens' in South Africa. My heart ached for the poor women, black, mostly, who were trapped in poverty – a life sentence without parole.

The idea that someone would read *Forced to Grow* and follow suit, do as I had done, slowly crept into my mind. I am a teacher by profession, and I know that, of all the jobs I have ever done, that is the one I believe I am most fitted to. It is the job I most enjoyed and would gladly go back to – if circumstances required this or permitted.

I don't know that a reader might not find the book almost like a 'How To' book, somewhat prescriptive. The decisions I took, what I believed they would lead to, successes and failures of those decisions and plans … it is all laid out there.

Who was I writing this book for, now that I was no longer just writing for future readers?

The answer is simple: for anyone who needed help in becoming what they were meant to be. For anyone who had somehow lost their way, found themselves to be a self very different from the one they had thought they would be when they were growing up.

Growing up, I had had dreams; all shattered before I hit twenty. But by the time I was writing *Forced to Grow*, not only had those dreams become reality, I had exceeded them. The life I was living was a life I could not have had in my dreams.

Along the way, I had hit a snag (or several). But the plight of my children forced me to pull myself up by my bootstraps – even though I had no boots. I was forced to find my way out of poverty and hopelessness, the alternative too gruesome to contemplate …

This was the possibility I presented to readers. This is what the book (or the author) hoped to convey. The gift my life gave, not only to me, but to others, is that I come of very humble stock. Anyone might be excused for looking at what my life has become and telling themselves: If *she* could do it, so can I!

10.
WHY I WROTE *MOTHER TO MOTHER*

This previously unpublished essay explains the genesis of this powerful novel about the turbulent period leading up to South Africa's first democratic elections in 1994. It narrates Sindiwe Magona's personal response to an event that brought South Africa much negative international attention – the 1993 killing of a 26-year-old Fulbright scholar from the United States by a group of young anti-apartheid protesters – and helps to explain why the novel continues to resonate with readers today.

MOTHER TO MOTHER (1998) is fiction, but there is no denying it is based on a real event, the murder of American Fulbright scholar, Amy Elizabeth Biehl, on 25 August 1993.

When that horrific event happened, I was not even in South Africa. I was in New York, USA, where I was working for the United Nations Organization, in the Department of Public Information (DPI). The tragic news spread internationally. That very same day, it reached us in New York. I didn't suddenly exclaim: Ah! There's a novel for me to write. In fact, I did not start writing *Mother to Mother* until 1996 – three full years after the event.

However, I was terribly saddened and felt deeply for the Biehl family, people I had no reason to believe I would ever meet. This is a typical response upon hearing sad news like this. When incidents such as these happen, how many of us do more than feel sorry for the families of the victims?

Eight months after Amy's murder, in April 1994, I was in South Africa to witness the miracle of the first democratic elections in the country. On the evening of my departure, Lindiwe Madikwa, a friend from primary-school days, drove me to the airport. That was before the 'Drop and Go' of today, when you could still drive your friend to the airport, go in and watch them check in, and, time permitting, have a bite in one of the cafés. Lindiwe and I did precisely that. She being a stickler for punctuality, I was a whole mile and a half early for my flight.

Over coffee we chatted about this and that, went over the miraculous happenings in the country, the 'everybody' elections no one had ever dreamed they would see. But, of course, the darker side of the life of the nation came up, with the Amy Biehl story at the fore; the four young men implicated in her murder were on trial. Lindiwe said to me: 'Do you know that one of those four boys is Nontuthuzelo's son?'

Ice-cold water, a bucketful, poured over me. 'Which Nontuthuzelo?' Mind-numb, I heard a voice croak. Between the two of us, there was only one Nontuthuzelo we knew – from our childhood days in Blouvlei. We were in the same class, played together, our homes in the same area: Blouvlei, a tin-shack 'location' as residential areas for black Africans were called then.

Nontuthuzelo fell pregnant around Standard Five (Grade 7) and had to leave school, that being the punishment meted out. She never recovered and is a typical example of what I call, elsewhere in my writing, 'a perfect product of apartheid'. Hers was the 'natural' status of the majority of Africans in apartheid South Africa – deliberate, designed, inescapable destitution.

My mind was reeled back by Lindiwe's 'Nontuthuzelo … Nontuthuzelo', nodding her head vigorously as if questioning my sanity in asking such a stupid question. Which Nontuthuzelo could it be other than the one we both knew? The one she vehemently painted into my numbed brain, which slowly crawled back from that space, that time – back to the here and now.

But I did not say: Aha! There's my novel! Instead I asked, 'How is she coping?'

That question surprised me. '*Coping*?' Did this apply to people whose children went about killing other people's children? Wasn't 'coping' the onerous, unenviable burden of the bereaved?

But something inside me had shifted. For the very first time in my life, in my fifties, I felt sorry for the parent of a killer.

I was still not writing a book about it; not even writing an article or a letter to the press, to say nothing of a card of condolence to the family who had lost a child. However, for two whole years following that unwanted intimate knowledge, I was pregnant with sorrow for that lost life … Nontuthuzelo's life. Bazooka-ed by apartheid. She had been such a spunky girl from age eight to fourteen. Then the birth of her son aborted whoever the person she herself would have become.

Oh, I still felt sorry for the Biehls. But now I also felt sorry for Nontuthuzelo. Therefore, although I did not know it at the time, a new thought was born in my mind the night I heard the news: The parents of murderers don't go on picnics! And, in a way, theirs is a harder row to hoe, for they know they do not have society's sympathy. They know we may even blame them for the actions of their children. Are we not all programmed by society to empathise with the families of victims? But then, what does society teach us about the flip side of such a tragedy? About the family of the perpetrator, the killer?

Nontuthuzelo's pain stayed with me; it made me see my life with fresh eyes. Not for the first time, I realised just how singularly fortunate I have been. One of those boys could so easily have been my son. Nontuthuzelo and I come from the same background; what had made our lives so markedly different today is opportunity – the chance of an education; more happenstance than design!

The very same circumstances as my own had given Nontuthuzelo and her son a life that would eventually lead to the murder of Amy Biehl. This realisation made me see that what had *really* killed Amy Biehl was apartheid. Yes, the four 'boys' who were arrested and charged with her murder had committed the gruesome act. But, to me, they were mere instruments. The real killer, the murderer who felled Amy Elizabeth Biehl, was the racial hatred we, *all* of us South Africans, allowed to flourish in society. We had all killed her – by allowing race hate to reach such levels and calling it 'our way of life'.

In the tradition of my people, amaXhosa, when such a thing happens, when one family wrongs another in such a grievous manner, irrespective of what happens in the court of law, the family of the perpetrator is obligated to take itself to the other family, the people it has wronged or aggrieved. Go there and make amends, ask for pardon from this family.

The Nontuthuzelo I once knew was zestful, witty and far from shy. I knew she would want to go to the victim's mother, Amy's mother. I knew she would want to observe this humane manner of making amends, irrespective of what the court of law decided. She would want to eyeball the mother of the dead child, mother to mother, and speak words of apology, of consolation, to her. This would, of course, not bring the dead back to life, but it would put a human face, a human heart, before the aggrieved family; help that family see that the monster who had killed their loved one was, despite such a monstrous act, a human being. Yes, lost, but still a human being.

But even as I saw, in my mind's eye, Nontuthuzelo approach the other mother, the limitations of distance, language, and culture presented as clear and present problems.

Still, the idea that Nontuthuzelo might want to approach Amy's mother would not leave me. In fact, it grew! I saw that, indeed, Amy's mother needed this encounter. She needed to hear from the other mother, the mother of her daughter's killer. I saw that, since I had come to see, very clearly, that we, all of us South Africans, black and white, killed Amy Biehl collectively, by allowing race hate to reach the levels it did … this was knowledge that Amy's mother needed to have. Her child had died because of apartheid. Apartheid killed her.

My burning desire was that Amy's mother should understand the race hate, legalised and accepted as 'our way of life' by those it benefitted, was loathed by those it subjugated; it had killed her daughter. But despite this desire, I did not make any overtures to Mrs Biehl. I tend to be very much on the timid side.

But the sense that she should know, *understand*, the underlying feelings, the racial hatred that were 'our way of life' eventually forced me to put down on paper what I believed were Nontuthuzelo's feelings. What I felt that, given the opportunity, she might say to Mrs Biehl. What I felt Mrs Biehl should understand about the nature of South Africa and its people.

So, I wrote *Mother to Mother* – a novel – comprising the fictionalised words of the mother of the killer to the mother of the victim, the words of the mother of one of the four young men who were tried and convicted of the murder of Amy Biehl. Imagined words, of course; but heartfelt nevertheless.

But then my son had not killed anybody. Therefore, the anguish that pours from the mother's heart in the book, from the mouth of the killer's mother – that is the product of my imagination. It is the product of empathy – putting myself in the shoes of the other – that and imagination. These are some of the tools that writers use: empathy and imagination. These, and the very hard work of the soul, produced my novel, *Mother to Mother*.

Writing this novel was far from easy. It would be three years after hearing of the involvement of a childhood friend in that tragic event before I put pen to paper. But first, I had to find a way to start the novel. It is one thing having an idea about a novel and quite another to create, to give birth to the complete work. But I had the good sense and courage, eventually, to get help.

When I saw a flyer about an upcoming workshop, 'for Advanced Novel Writing', I leapt at the chance, never mind that I did not quite meet the specifications. Not only was I not in the 'advanced' category of novel writing, I had not even written one sentence. But desperate situations call for desperate measures.

I applied and was accepted to attend the six-week workshop, which was to be held at the 96th Street YMCA in New York. The workshop leader was Arthur Flowers, a prominent and generous writer. We were to meet on Saturday mornings for a period of six weeks. The flyer stipulated: 'Bring an outline or first chapter of your novel to the first meeting'. I went with nothing on paper and only the barest of ideas in my mind.

When Arthur asked us to introduce ourselves, the formula was: name, title of novel and why you felt the world needed it. When my turn came, I said:

> I'm Sindiwe Magona, from South Africa. My country is dealing with a horrendous past and trying to knit itself into a nation. To do that, it needs to undergo a process of reconciliation. I'm going to write a novel on reconciliation because reconciliation is vital to the continuation of human existence. As a species, we could not survive if we had not learned the art of healing, forgiving, and going on – living, despite past hurts. We need to forgive ourselves, forgive others. The title of my novel is *Mother to Mother* and the novel will be the words of the mother of the killer to the mother of the victim.

A sigh arose from the group. I got the feeling I had hit on a very good idea.

Arthur gave us homework, which we had to bring the following Saturday: a complete outline – few had done that! – or the first chapter.

Elated and encouraged at the reception of my 'idea' – I went home and, that afternoon, wrote out all my pent-up feelings about Nontuthuzelo's grief which had lived inside me since that long-ago evening when Lindiwe had told me: 'Do you know, one of those four boys is Nontuthuzelo's son?'

When, the following Saturday, I read out what I had written, the group was spellbound. Well, four Saturdays later, we hit the end of the workshop, but I still had only forty-odd pages to my name. I had poured out all the pain, the grief, the bewilderment I felt Nontuthuzelo must have undergone that first shocked night the awful news confronted her, assaulted her, imprisoning her very soul.

He bade each of the participants adieu, and when my turn came, Arthur Flowers implored, 'Write the novel, Sindiwe, please!' But now that I had purged the grief, Nontuthuzelo's grief, I had absolutely nothing more to say. For months and months, the 'novel' remained that sorry-looking, rather flat file on my desk. That file, coupled with the urgings of Arthur Flowers, now and then pricked my conscience; but the courage to continue, get down to the serious business of confronting that blank sheet of paper and spoil it with words dug up from deep inside me, words unknown to me, terrible words that, once put down, became their own, mistresses of their destiny, totally independent, with no strings attached to even she who thought she was source from which they had sprung – that courage was hard to summon, hard, for the likes of me.

Eventually, the faith of my late son, Sandile Soyiso Sayedwa, in my ability to accomplish the feat, write the novel *Mother to Mother*, about which I had, of course, told my family, opened me up and tore the words out my fear-frozen heart. Sandile had tirelessly sent me clippings from South Africa. And so it was that, long months after the workshop run by Arthur Flowers, I revisited the novel. And yet, even then, it never occurred to me I could interview either the Biehls or Nontuthuzelo – timidity again!

Because I knew some of Nontuthuzelo's personal history, having lived in the same vicinity when we were children of primary-school age, and I had occasionally bumped into her later on, in our late twenties, I fashioned some of the back story. The events of the murder, well documented, provided most of the actuality. The rest, as they say, is 'creative writing'.

When I wrote *Mother to Mother* I'd already had four books published: two books of autobiography –*To My Children's Children* (1990) and *Forced to Grow* (1992), and two books of short stories – *Living, Loving, and Lying Awake at Night* (1991) and *Push-Push! and Other Stories* (1996), all published by David Philip Publishers. It figures, then, that I presented the manuscript to the same publisher, and, to my delight, Marie Philip accepted it.

In June 1998, while I was on home leave from the United Nations Organization, the publisher took the opportunity of doing a final edit of the book, which was due out in September that year. But now, belatedly, the spectre of the interviews I had so scrupulously avoided rose. Though this was not something that had never occurred to me, my heart still dropped when Marie Philip pointed out it would be awkward to have the book hit the bookstores without having had a word with the people concerned. 'After all', she said, 'this is recent history'.

Even *bangbroek*[1] me could see the validity of Marie's assertion. Much as I was petrified of meeting especially the Biehls, I was even more frightened, and knew I would be deeply ashamed, if I refused. I could not think of a more insulting thing, adding to the injury the Biehl family had suffered at the hands of my country, my nation. Reluctantly, I made an appointment, and a few days later I met the now deceased Peter Biehl, Amy's father, who listened to my story.

Peter Biehl was huge – or so he seemed to me, especially that morning of the first day I met him. I was scared going to meet him but, upon seeing him towering on the other side of the desk across which he stonily eyed me, I became petrified. I quickly pushed my four previously published books across his desk as I garbled something to the effect of, 'I'm a published author. I've now written a novel based on the …' Here, I got stuck. How could I say 'the murder of your child? Amy's story?' I no longer recall what, exactly, I did say before ending with: 'The book is about to be published'.

The only comment the man made was to ask whether the publisher could give him a copy. I hastily assured Mr Biehl that this could be arranged. I was certain that David and Marie Philip would have no problem with that. Peter asked when the book was due and I replied, 'Sometime in September'. He immediately requested that I ask the publisher to consider launching in August, on the date that Amy had died, and I promised to convey his message. Although I gave no guarantees, I was quite certain the publisher would have no objection to that request either.

'Shall we get a cup of coffee?' Peter Biehl said quietly.

Was the man insane? Quaking in my boots as I was, I had absolutely no intention of prolonging a visit I had undertaken with the greatest reluctance, feeling extremely uncomfortable, awkward throughout. I hastily responded, 'I'm afraid I must rush off … I've another meeting', and I scooted out of his office. There was in fact no scheduled meeting. But I was going to see Nontuthuzelo in Gugulethu, bringing the same four books I had thrown onto Peter Biehl's desk that morning. I felt I owed her at least that – so that she would know of the writing I had done, as well as the whys and wherefores.

David Philip Publishers without hesitation agreed to Peter Biehl's request. They sent off a complimentary copy of my new novel, and *Mother to Mother* was released on 25 August 1998 – five years to the day after that awful event. The magnanimity of the Biehl family is today widely acknowledged.

Weeks after that meeting with Peter Biehl, my phone rang at my office in New York. 'UN DPI', I answered.

'This is Peter Biehl', said a quietly confident voice, and I immediately collapsed back onto the chair from which I had sprung to answer the phone on the far side of the desk.

'Yes?' I croaked as my knees shook.

'We got the book.'

'Yes?' My voice had gone down several decibels; the trembling was spreading to other parts of my body.

'We read the book', he very deliberately articulated. I swallowed hard before repeating 'Yes', realising even as I said it that this word had suddenly become the only one in my shrunken vocabulary – all the while, the volume of my voice diminishing, disappearing. I was almost whispering by now.

In a booming voice, Peter declared, 'We loved the book!'

I think I must have blacked out for a second or two. Next thing I knew, bells were ringing in my ears as I heard the voice saying, 'We bought thirty copies and have given them to friends'. Then, triumphantly, the cheery voice announced, 'Archbishop Tutu has a copy!'

Why didn't you say that from the beginning? You nearly killed me, you know? Aloud, I said, 'Why, thank you! Thank you, very much!' I'm sure Peter Biehl thought I was thanking him, thanking his entire family, for not taking offence at what I had written, at the sheer presumptuousness of writing a book based on their sad loss.

My thanks were, however, aimed at the Almighty, at God, the Universe, for such huge and selfless hearts which the Biehl family showed South Africa and the world. Peter and Linda Biehl, Amy's parents, came to South Africa to see for themselves the place that had taken their loved one, their daughter, from them – taken her in such a tragic, cruel and senseless way. And what they did after that told the world who Amy Elizabeth Biehl really was. Children do not raise themselves. Amy did not. She was the big heart she was because, to a large extent, she had the parents she had. Kindness, understanding, integrity, love of your fellow man, values that guide humanity when we live principled lives – the Biehl family exhibited these in the manner of their reaction to the tragedy, how we should live in and through those principles. They saw what had led to the killing of their child, the poverty and hopelessness that blights the lives of millions of young people in South Africa, and they found it in their hearts to do something that would increase the chances of some of those unfortunate people to escape the fate life had bequeathed them.

The Amy Biehl Foundation[2] opened within months of Amy's death. It is a youth-outreach NGO with an after-school programme for children in various poorly-serviced townships and informal settlements in the Cape Town vicinity. Such is the generosity the Biehls showed, not only to South Africans but also to the world. There they were, dealing with the worst nightmare parents can have. And yet, instead of rage and hate, instead of acts of revenge and the like – justifiable behaviours that the wronged often exhibit – this family set upon a different path, a path of healing. They were about helping the very people, the very country, that had killed their daughter, so that they might live worthwhile lives. In other words, the Biehl family was looking at the root causes of the poison that had taken their loved one's life. And that is what they chose to deal with: not the symptom, but the radical cause, the core.

In the meantime, my book was out and critics were having a field day. Yes, there was praise for *Mother to Mother*. But there were also reviewers who wanted to know what colour of animal this writer was. How did she dare write a novel about this tragedy? I am happy to report that even such critics, people who approached the book with misgivings, horror even, came round, ultimately seeing merit in the book. For this I was grateful – very grateful.

In December 1998, the General Assembly of the United Nations Organization asked Linda and Peter Biehl to address it on Human Rights Day – 10 December. The couple agreed, with the proviso that I be part of the ensuing panel discussion: Human Rights in Southern Africa. It was very well received.

Afterwards, the Biehls and I had lunch together at a Japanese restaurant near the UN. Linda had not yet finished reading the book, she confessed: 'I find it hard in places'. I assured her that I completely understood; I, too, found it hard in places. Hard to read; and it had been hard to write. To this day, there are parts of the book that bring tears to my eyes. Not every time I read those parts, but sometimes, as I read, the senseless loss of such a young and promising life overwhelms me, and I weep.

Some months after this meeting with the Biehls, they came to New York City again. And again they got in touch. Would I do lunch with them, they wanted to know? Would I?

At lunch, at the same restaurant, Linda surprised me. She had now read the book from beginning to end. 'And', she said softly. 'It helped me better understand'. If you'd told me I had won the Pulitzer Prize, I could not have been more pleased, or happier. To this day, when I recall that moment, Linda telling me what the book had done for her, the warm feeling that washed all over me returns, I feel it anew. The book had achieved what I had set out to do, barely perceived even by me at the beginning, an overwhelming sense that this other mother, the dead child's mother, should see, understand, that her child died because of apartheid. She had died because we, the people of South Africa, all of us, black and white, had allowed race hate to rise to such a level that it governed our collective national heart. Yes, Mxolisi[3] and three other young men had killed Amy Biehl, but it was the whole nation who had killed her. The murder of Amy Biehl is a national crime, a national sin.

I had started the project on first hearing of the involvement of someone I'd once known – with whom I had played as a child – in something so tragic, so unfathomable. I had grieved for her, for the bleak predicament in which she found herself. 'How is she coping?' I'd asked Lindiwe that long ago night as I waited to board the Pan Am flight to New York, going back to my job at the United Nations. The book had grown in me, first as the grief I felt for Nontuthuzelo, stuck there with no way of escaping the sad reality that her son had killed an innocent woman for no reason at all. However, in the course of writing *Mother to Mother* I began to see how I was a Nontuthuzelo too. I shared in the culpability of the deed – as all South Africans do. For what happens in our countries happens because we, the people, do not do all we can do to stop the growth of rot, of evil, of crime. The book was provoked by all these issues. Thank you, Marie Philip – it was that gentle woman, my very first editor, who gave me the word 'provoked' – a word I have used many times as it best explains why I write the books I write. It was not the grotesque murder of Amy Elizabeth Biehl that inspired me. It was when I came to know more about the circumstances and characters involved that I became more intimately involved with the tragic event. That identification, that empathy, is what finally 'provoked' me to put pen to paper, and out came the story – *Mother to Mother*!

That the Biehl family could respond to their tragic loss with the creation of a foundation to help them deal with that loss should give us cause to pause. For that is the work our nation – we, the South African nation – has neglected. Not only the extent but also the gruesome nature of crime all around us is evidence of that.

The four young men implicated in Amy's murder were jailed for life. But then came the Truth and Reconciliation Commission, and the Biehls did not oppose their application to appear before it. The boys were pardoned; their crime deemed a political act. Peter Biehl was quoted in the *New York Times* immediately afterwards, saying that he hoped society would give these young men the support they needed so that they might live worthwhile lives.

These are words South Africans should never forget. Moreover, they are words we as a nation should take to heart, letting them guide us towards action that achieves this aim – not only in the lives of those four 'young men' but in the lives of all the children of this nation. Only then will the future of this nation be secured.

I was humbled when, after the death of Peter Biehl, the family asked me to deliver a eulogy at his memorial service at the National Cathedral in Washington, D.C. If there is one lesson I have learnt from my involvement with the story of Amy Biehl, it is that there are no 'them' and 'us'. All humanity is one as, indeed, all creation is one.

11.
WHY I WROTE *BEAUTY'S GIFT*

In this revised essay, which was published under the same title as the introduction to the Pan Macmillan reprint of Beauty's Gift *in 2018, Sindiwe Magona describes coming to terms with the severity of the HIV and Aids crisis in South Africa, and giving herself permission to write a novel about the vulnerability of middle-class (black) married women to the virus due to the infidelity of their male partners.*

SEVERAL CONSIDERATIONS WENT into the decision to return to my home country, South Africa, from my extended stay in the United States of America. First and foremost, besides the fact that I missed home and my family, I recognised that my writing was rooted in South Africa and things South African. I felt I needed to reconnect, be 'on the spot', as it were, so as to be more in tune with what was happening in the country day-to-day, rather than relying on reportage. I seemed to be bombarded daily with reports of the raging fire in the country of my birth – a veritable catastrophe that was laying waste to all life, especially young life. But this was a consideration I acknowledged mostly unconsciously, as I didn't say to myself: I'm going home to join the fight against HIV and Aids. Yet the pandemic troubled me to the core of my being.

In the early days, when Aids was still but a rumour, I attended my first Aids conference in the early 1990s in New York. A South African nurse, Nonceba Lubanga, had organised this. At the time, I knew very little about the disease. That was the time we still held the mistaken notion it was something that killed gay men. The only reason I attended the conference, held over a weekend, was because Nonceba is not only a loyal friend but one of those people you don't say no to – you'd better do as she says, or else ...

What I learnt from that conference left me numb. Looking back, I know I had still not grasped the magnitude of what was about to befall us. I remember the spine-chilling words: 'By the year 2000, there will hardly be a family, in South Africa, not touched by Aids ...'. Hardly a family ...

I can still recall the palpable, overwhelming sense of doom with which I left the conference. I do not remember ever being so scared in my entire life.

But did I do anything? Anything that could have averted the disaster? I'm not saying I could have. I'm not saying that any one person could have done that. But where's the harm in trying? Yet all I did, in my bewilderment, was picture which of my nieces or nephews might be affected. In my mind's eye I'd see them all and wonder: Will it be this one? Or that one?

Can you believe how stupid I was? How ill-informed? Who had told me the disease would pick only *one* member, per family? That the plague should be that considerate, that mindful of our folly, that courteous? But I utterly lacked the capacity to imagine the workings of a plague. And all I did – the full extent of my preventive measures – was to mail home some of the handouts I'd received at the conference. I sent them with the instruction: 'READ THIS AND PAY HEED!'

Reports on the scourge were alarming: 'We are losing more people in South Africa today than would be the case were we at war'. This said a lot about the sorry state in which we found ourselves, not only in South Africa but throughout the continent of Africa in all its vastness.

Thinking about this, the damage Aids was wreaking, I wondered at our being, in Africa, forever prone to tragedy: plagues and disasters, whether man-made or natural; warfare and other acts of man's inhumanity to man. All our countries in Africa seemed capable of doing nothing but the gross negative.

Around this time, I had attended a meeting of the young people in my street in Gugulethu. They wanted me to see the work they were doing and to find out if there was any way in which I could help them in their fight against crime. The Youth Club, as they called themselves, had also invited a nurse, a younger woman I knew quite well. Of course, the major obstacle to all the plans the Youth Club had was lack of funding. Lack of funding and lack of support. They were running the club as an informal group, with no office space or personnel. Nonetheless, I was impressed with what they were trying to achieve – their insightfulness and their obvious dedication to the cause.

It was during the coffee hour, a time to mingle and get refreshments provided by the host family, that the other invited guest asked the boys to 'please step outside for a minute' as she had something she wanted to 'say to the girls in private'. I listened. With growing amazement, I listened.

'Those of you who have already seen your moon time,' the woman continued, 'whether you are twelve or eleven, it doesn't matter, as long as you have started. I want you to tell your mother to bring you to the clinic, on a Wednesday.'

She asked the girls whether they knew where the clinic was. Many did, but she gave the address anyway, adding, 'Come on a Wednesday, when the only *sisi*[1] and mama who'll see you are the ones bringing girls for their first visit to the clinic'.

All this time, my mind was furiously at work. Why is she asking girls that young to go to the women's clinic, I wondered? But I didn't wonder for long. The woman explained to the girls: 'You must come and get an injection'.

But that's for birth control! my mind screamed in protest, absolutely horrified. These girls were so young. And the woman was asking them to come … as young as eleven or twelve … why?

'So that when you are raped, you won't get pregnant.'

The woman's explanation horrified me even more.

'Most of these girls know they will be raped ... sooner or later', she explained, no doubt seeing the confusion and bewilderment written on my brow. The girls were also advised to insist their boyfriends used condoms. The woman told them, too, that regular attendance at the clinic would help them to get the advice they needed if they were too shy to ask their mothers or caregivers.

What on earth is the matter with us, my people? How did we end up where we are? Where little girls grow up with the certainty that they'll be raped? Grow up with warnings. Grow up following dread-filled advice. For that is what it is when children are advised to take drugs so they will not fall pregnant when they are raped. *These girls know they will be raped* – a categorical statement relating to their future ... What of the morrow, then? What does such a statement say about our tomorrow, about what we, South Africans, have to look forward to?

I had not been in the country one day before the dreadful reports about the virus were confirmed over and over again. I listened as one person after another told me of the ravages of the disease. Yes, I had heard these stories while I was in New York. But this was different. Now, I was getting the hard news first-hand. Or, at the very least, second-hand.

My best friend, Faith, who had picked me up at the airport, came to see me the next day. There was nothing unusual about that. She had always done so whenever I was home. Indeed, besides my immediate family, I can say she is the person with whom I spent the most time whenever I was home, on holiday. Now, we exchanged the usual pleasantries.

Then Faith said quietly, 'People are dying like flies here, Sindi. Everywhere you go, you hear the same lamentation – "Our children are all dying! What are we to do? Who will look after us in our old age?"'. Then, her voice rising, she said, 'And now, one of my nieces, Vuyi, is down with a severe cold that just won't let up. I am so worried!'

'Do you think she might be HIV positive?'

'Who can say, my friend? Today, you can't tell the young people anything. They believe they know more than you.'

The young lady would show signs of improvement, and their alarm would diminish. 'But it's been an on-again, off-again affair. So much so, she has lost her job.'

I asked whether Faith's niece had seen a doctor.

'With what? Her employer didn't give her health insurance.'

Vuyi had worked for the company for a full nineteen years, Faith went on to tell me. I expressed my sympathy and told her I'd come see Vuyi. I had brought a black doll for her six-year-old daughter, Linda, which I'd named after me.

'That will cheer her up. And it will certainly cheer little Linda no end.' Faith stopped, hung her head and said, 'She is so bright – our little Linda. So bright, my heart aches for her. What would happen to her if …'

Two days later, 'if' became reality: 'Vuyi passed away two hours ago.'

It was not till well after eight that evening that I finally got a chance to be alone with Faith. It was then that she explained everything to me; made me understand. Her niece had not wanted her status made public. 'And one has to respect the wishes of the sufferer.' That was understandable. Years ago, a young woman in KwaZulu-Natal had been stoned to death by her community for doing exactly that. Elsewhere in the world, people were scared of the stigma attached to being an HIV-positive patient; in South Africa, one risked summary execution by revealing one's status.

Vuyi had also lacked the medical attention she needed because she had no medical cover, despite being employed. She, like so many HIV-positive people, had died – and were dying and would continue dying – because they received no treatment at all. Either they could not afford to be tested, being too poor to go to a doctor or, having been diagnosed, they could not afford the drugs prescribed.

I found myself thinking: What a pity the country was not struck by a major earthquake or some other natural disaster of equal magnitude. A tsunami, perhaps. Guess what would have happened then? Without all this bureaucratic crap, dozens of countries would have flocked to South Africa, offering millions of dollars as unconditional aid. No questions asked, we would have received financial aid, and armies would have come to lend a hand. Goods – foodstuffs, clothing and other requisite materials – would have been flown to South Africa. Alas, we did not suffer an earthquake. But, believe me, the disaster facing us will have outcomes more far-reaching than those from any natural disaster of whatever scale.

Then, to make matters worse, we had government spokesmen make public statements that would have had them recalled elsewhere in the world. Recalled the very next day following their vile statements to the press. A few days before Vuyi's passing, for example, I'd watched a man on TV justifying the government's refusal to give antiretroviral drugs to expectant mothers, which could prevent in utero infection.

'We all know these women are going to die,' he said, adding, 'and what is the government to do with all these orphans?'

I couldn't believe I'd heard what I knew I'd just heard. Was the fool drunk? On some brain-numbing drugs? How could he make such a callous statement? And do so on behalf of the government! I was sure he would lose his position the very next day. The government would disassociate itself from such unworthy talk – talk amounting to a condonement of the worst kind of genocide, the killing of innocents. For what can be more innocent, more vulnerable, than the human embryo? But no, let us allow them to get infected so that they, along with their already sick mothers, can die. That is what the government spokesman was saying, any way you looked at it. It was – what? Cheaper for the government to allow thousands of children to be born HIV-positive, to live their short, miserable lives, and die young... This was cheaper? Cheaper than saving these lives, for doing so would then saddle the government with the terrible burden of looking after them.

Till the day I die, I will never comprehend the cruelty, the callousness, the total disregard for human life contained in the man's statement. There were no repercussions, and, not long afterwards, the man himself died of natural causes. We deserve better from our government. South Africa deserves better, far better.

I was pleasantly surprised, after my initial shock, when Faith told me the family had decided to reveal Vuyi's status, that she'd been HIV-positive. This does not mean *I* was not hesitant, reluctant and downright scared. Then my friend asked me to be one of the speakers at her niece's funeral. My heart plummeted as my whole body turned to rubber! Swift to follow was a wave of shame. I was struck by the huge courage this family displayed, even at that stage. To come out and announce or admit such a thing was an act of great bravery. What was I being asked to do? What was giving a speech compared to the death of the young woman? Compared to this grieving family, who were risking ridicule and public shaming to help other sufferers and their families, to help those not yet infected, to increase awareness ... and here I was, a grown woman knocking at the door of retirement, and I flinched at the thought of delivering an address.

'Thank you, friend. That will be my honour!' I was not joking, I meant it. I had recovered my senses – what little I still possessed.

The first speaker at the funeral was a woman who had lived with HIV for more than ten years. An African, she was considerably older than what appeared to be the norm for HIV and Aids-related illnesses – women under thirty. But then, when I considered how long she had had the condition, I realised I was looking at a survivor. She, too, must have been under thirty when first diagnosed. But now, I put her in her late thirties, perhaps forty. She couldn't be a day older than forty, I guessed.

The address I gave was widely hailed as being sorely needed by the community. Indeed, many teachers present asked for a copy afterwards. I promised to send the speech to Faith, who would make copies to give to those who wanted one. But I later heard that requests were made by some who were not impressed with my speech, asking, 'Isn't she criticising the government?'

Regarding those who heard criticism of the government in the address, of course my immediate reaction was to worry that I would be in danger if I was seen to be anti-government! For, during the apartheid era, saying anything critical of the government was asking for jail. Now, I can only hope our people have learnt a lesson from that experience. That pointing out mistakes made by those in power does not automatically make you an enemy of the government. If the government cannot be criticised by the people it purports to represent, by the people it serves – or is supposed to serve – then where is this power that is supposed to be in the hands of the people? Isn't that what democracy means? A government of the people, by the people, for the people? Where, then, is the crime, should the people inquire of those representing them: How come? Why? We need to ask ourselves: Do our representatives not owe us an explanation? How else will we discover how well they are doing their job, serving us, the people? These questions lead to even more important questions: How will they know whether we are happy or not with their performance? Do they not need our feedback? Should they not give us answers when we have questions? Should such questions automatically be considered an attack on government?

Despite my initial misgivings about my speech, I knew that I had every right to question the government. The assumption that I do not have this right is a reminder of the real danger: the fear most of us still harbour in our hearts, that displeasing the government, any government, has dire repercussions. Such an assumption courts danger. Whenever this happens, anywhere in the world, those in power have succeeded in shielding themselves from scrutiny; then they are free to do as they please, with little regard for the people they claim to serve. And that spells death to any semblance of democracy. In such a situation, that disregard for truth sets the tone for the rest of the community, for the nation.

Let's have a look at what that old, rather tired, definition actually says: Democracy is government of the people, by the people, for the people. All very well … except, which people? Everyone in the country? Or only those who support the ruling party? Yet even there, is it just the in-group that matters, whose interests are catered to? This might sound like a trite question. But for people who come from many traditions of exclusion (political, gender, language group, age, disability, geographical origins, to name but some) it is not always clear that one is invited to the party. And even when this complaint is voiced, it is not easy to accept that as fact, never mind own it to the extent one acts on it.

But, to introduce an analogy that might prove helpful here, sending a child to the shop is something we, Africans, know very well. It is part of who we are, of our ways of doing things, and living in a democracy is like sending a child to the shop. The parent wants something – bread, for instance. She knows exactly what kind of bread she wants; how much of it she wants; and how much it costs. What is more, she knows which of her children would be best to send, especially if what she wants is important or expensive or she is in a hurry for it, for example, yeast, after she has already mixed the flour, salt, sugar, milk and eggs. That is why she calls on the child she trusts to do what she wants done – to do it right.

She explains to the child clearly what it is she wants from the shop. She gives the child the money. She knows whether the money is just enough or whether there will be any change. She knows how long it takes the child to get to the shop and back. And the child knows that the mother knows how long the trip should take; whether she expects change, expecting to receive the correct item and the correct number – for example, two loaves of brown bread.

Now, both parent and child have the same knowledge: what to buy, and what quantity; how much it will cost; and how long the trip to the shop will take.

The child also knows that the parent will be displeased should the wrong article be bought or incorrect change be given or the trip takes longer than expected. What is more, the child knows that there will be a price to pay if any of this happens. The parent has explained that and may, indeed, remind the child of this.

Also, both know the parent is keeping watch. The parent does not call the child and give him the money and tell him what he must buy from the shop and then promptly forget about sending him to the shop. To the contrary, her expectation occupies her until the child returns. The child who brings the required item is rewarded. The child who returns with the wrong item or loses the change or takes too long is punished. The mother will not fail to show her displeasure.

That is how real democracy works. And that is what we do when we vote. The vote is our money. We give that money to the people we send to parliament. We send them there so that they can give us what we need. They go there to make sure we get what we need. It is important, therefore, that we tell them exactly what it is we want – what we expect them to get for us. We must know what we want. We must send only those people we trust to do what we want done. Importantly, we need to work together if we are to succeed in doing the work of the nation.

The members of parliament are sent there by us – all of the people who cast their vote. They are our servants. We send them to work for all of us. But, like the mother who sends her child to the shop, it is very important that we – *all* the voters – ensure that the people we send to parliament are doing what we sent them there to do. This is the crux of democracy. Going to vote every five years or so is not enough. That vote is power; the only power we have as citizens in a democracy. However, we need to pay attention after we have voted. You see, when we vote, it's like sending a child we trust to the shop. We expect them to return with the goods we ordered.

We should always keep our eyes on our servants. Are they doing what we asked of them? Are they doing their jobs to the best of their ability? Are they overspending? Or spending on the wrong things? Are they taking much longer than expected to deliver the services we'd sent them to parliament for in the first place?

That way, we use our power, our vote, to ensure that civil servants always remember that they are where they are simply to serve us, the people. If we do not use this power, civil servants may forget that they are the servants of the people and start behaving as though they were better than the people who sent them to parliament. When that happens, democracy no longer lives in that country. It is dead, and what you get is a pretend democracy and the people live in fear of their government. In a real democracy, it is the government that lives in fear of the people!

Having voiced my strong opinions about the government's response to the crisis at the funeral of Faith's niece, I began to develop my ideas about the role that male infidelity and gender-based violence play in women's extreme vulnerability to Aids, and my conclusions would eventually – after much hesitation on my part – make their way into my novel *Beauty's Gift* (2008).

The callous and unjust treatment of women in South Africa was first brought home to me by the case of a young woman whose husband was negligent of his duties and obligations as husband and head of the family, as well as being a well-known playboy. His wife died.

Although her family had realised even before this that she had full-blown Aids, they chose not to disclose her status, fearing that people would call her a 'slut', even though it was a well-known fact that she was not. It was also known to all who knew this family that her husband was a township 'player' who had several 'first-borns', that is, children who were his first-borns with whatever woman he'd impregnated. Faithful to him despite his many indiscretions, his wife had died of Aids. Her family, understandably, was inconsolable. Distant relatives, they had my sympathy. This was one of those episodes that has never left me.

But the turning point came when I heard a question asked by a woman minister at the Synod of the Church of the Province of Southern Africa in 2009.

'Your Grace,' she asked, 'what must I say to a woman who comes to me weeping and asks, "Mfundisi, why is God doing this to me? I married my husband when I was twenty-two and have never slept with another man; but now I have Aids!'" She went on to say, 'Faithfully married women are dying of Aids!'

In a flash, Beauty's face appeared before me: the story came to me, rather than my discovering it!

Fear, as I clearly saw in that moment, had held me back from writing a novel about HIV and Aids. Yes, I had done some writing about the issue: an unpublished essay, 'Like Sending a Child to the Shop'; a book of poetry, *Please, Take Photographs* (2009), and, that same year, a play, *Vukani! (Wake Up!)*. And I had given speeches – but there was no novel, although the issue never left me. Today, I ask myself, why I was so scared? The answer is simple, difficult to admit: in societies such as the one in which I grew up, people tend to be territorial about matters such as these.

I needed permission.

This may seem strange, odd. But my life was wholly circumscribed, as was that of my parents and their parents before them.

Still, those harrowing words from the woman priest at Synod, 'Faithfully married women are dying of Aids' freed me/unfroze me. Suddenly, I felt compelled to write the novel. Compelled and duty-bound.

In that way, then, *Beauty's Gift* is a book that chose me. For years I'd resisted writing it, for I was afraid. And the person I feared most was my brother, the black man; my son, the black man. I was afraid that black men would hate me for what I needed to say if I was going to be honest.

But outrage drove me to start the journey. Outrage at such wanton waste of life – death that could so easily be prevented. And the senseless murder of women through love, by the men they love.

Faithfully married women are dying of Aids.

Did black men love us, love the black women they killed? How did love kill women who served their men faithfully, seeing to all their needs?

A burning anger chased fear from my heart. Love should not kill. One's marriage certificate should not become one's death certificate. *Beauty's Gift* is a challenge to women to take charge of their lives, safeguard their lives, regard their lives as more precious than anything anyone promises or gives them, for nothing is more precious than one's life. Nothing. It is from living that all else ensues. Where is the great sex when you are no longer alive? The love? Money, or the big house, the car or beautiful clothes? Where are all those things when you are dead? Dead and buried? Nothing beats being alive – nothing!

Men who truly love women would not kill them. Love does not kill. It is not love when one recklessly endangers another.

Not a few of the 'faithfully married women [who] are dying of Aids' were known to me personally, or were known to my friends or neighbours. These were ordinary women, members of the emerging black middle class. They were professional women: teachers, nurses, social workers, lawyers and the like. However, the lie persisted that Aids afflicted poor women who, because they were utterly dependent on the financial support of the men in their lives, could not save themselves; could not say 'No!' to unprotected sex even when they knew the partner/husband was a player. Even when these women knew the men in their lives engaged in unprotected sex with multiple partners.

However, evidence abounded that women who were not dependent on men for a roof over their heads or bread on the table were also succumbing to the HIV and Aids pandemic. Just as, earlier in the scourge, it had been important, urgent, to dispel the myth that Aids was a disease of people who were gay, homosexuals, whom the gods were punishing for their 'iniquity' – so it was now crucial to dispel the myth that, in the black community, Aids killed only poor women. What supported that myth was the fact that professional women could afford, and gain access to, private medical care, thereby keeping their status private. Whereas their poorer sisters, forced to go to the clinics and day hospitals, stand in long queues, have their names called out over the public address system and told which window to go to collect their medication, had their status publicly exposed.

Knowledge is power. The African woman of professional status had to be apprised of the fact that she was in danger and that she was not alone in her predicament. This led to my decision, regarding my five female characters, that the women, if they were to serve the purpose of this particular novel, had to be far from poor; they had to be women who were in the professions, doing well, not experiencing debt stress. In other words, the reading public had to witness the self-deception women from this group often engage in, to their detriment, particularly in times of sexually-transmitted diseases, especially HIV and Aids.

But who were these women, and what were they about? That was the next question I asked myself. For there to be built-in trust among them, they needed to have known one another for a significant period of time and not be new acquaintances. Therefore, I chose not to make them colleagues at work or neighbours. A good place for first encounters seemed to be school. Since, before the advent of democracy in South Africa, black families were more or less cemented to their places of residence and did not move about, this appeared perfect. These women would have met in their first year of school and, although they might have gone their separate ways regarding high school and tertiary education, their families remained in the homes where they had grown up. Therefore, come holidays, the women would meet up again. And once they were done with whatever training they had undergone, they would, of course, start off living at home with their parents. With this being the usual trajectory of black life, I made these assumptions regarding my female characters. As young women who had grown up together and been friends 'forever', the novel would explore what their friendship might mean when one of them is dying of an Aids-related illness.

Women and friendship, what does that actually mean? What does it mean when, among other things, love comes into the picture? The love of a woman for her man, her lover or her husband: what does that translate to regarding her friends, her women friends. I remember stories of my younger self, how my friends and I lied to one another about our relationships. How we made the men in our lives out to be more than what they were – because we didn't want our friends to know the truth, fearing that that truth would diminish us in their eyes. That, if they knew, *really* knew, the men in our lives for who they were, what kind of men they in fact were, what they did or did not do, what we suffered and endured in our relationships, this would somehow lessen our standing in the eyes of our friends. Furthermore, such an admission would force a woman to admit what she had been at pains to hide, not just from others, but from herself too. Primarily from herself.

It is not easy for a woman to admit publicly that she is in an unsatisfying relationship, let alone admit she is in one that is abusive! How much more difficult, then, it is to admit to one's friends that one is in a toxic relationship – to say nothing of admitting that publicly? What is more, the not-poor women, the so-called middle-class women, have their status to safeguard. When everyone insists on talking of Aids as a disease which poor women are prone to because of their dependency on the men in their lives, what excuse will this woman, who is definitely not poor, give herself for staying in a relationship in which she knows her life is no longer safe? Her poorer sisters should surely not be expected to barter their very lives for a roof over their head and a loaf of bread – and she doesn't even have that sad excuse.

What does it take for a woman to say: 'I am a fool to be in this relationship. This relationship is not good for me. It hasn't been good for a long time. This relationship is killing me.'? For that is the realisation that dawns upon my character Beauty. This is no easy thing, as is shown by the fact that it is only in the final stages of her life, when she can no longer deny to herself that she is dying, that she reveals her HIV status. And this she does to only one of her friends, Amanda – a woman who belongs, as she does, to the Five Firm Friends or FFF Sisterhood. Beauty, Amanda, Cordelia, Edith and Doris are all professional women: capable, employed and self-sufficient. And yet, one of them succumbs to Aids.

The novel is a wake-up call to women, especially middle-class women lulled into a false sense of security by their wealth, forced into self-deception by their sense of shame when they are at the receiving end of the hateful acts of others – acts that kill, that lead to death, their own death.

Beauty's Gift is about friendship and courage, love and death during the Aids pandemic. When 'faithfully-married', 35-year-old Beauty falls ill and, after six short weeks, dies of an Aids-related illness, she defies the usual secrecy that so often surrounds such events. She urges her friend to tell her story to the other three members of the Sisterhood, to open their eyes to their vulnerability to HIV and Aids, so that they will not die an unnecessary death, as she soon will. With supreme courage, Beauty confides her secret, showing the women how loving blindly puts women in jeopardy. 'Live!' Beauty tells her friends, urging them not to 'die a stupid death like me!'

In this way, a woman's love for her four female friends, closer than sisters, becomes a vehicle for transforming her plight into a means for saving their lives – and ultimately into a book that spreads her instructive story.

Beauty's death starts a crusade, and the FFF (now Four Firm Friends) embark on the rest of their journey together, supporting one another – and that is vital. But the question remains: will their significant others follow or balk? For it is men as well as women who must take responsibility for staying alive, and not murder those they profess to love.

That is the story, the story of Beauty, which was birthed as a result of my return home at such an unfortunate moment in the life of my country.

12.
WHY I WROTE *CHASING THE TAILS OF MY FATHER'S CATTLE*

This previously unpublished essay explains Sindiwe Magona's turn to rural fiction in this novel, as well as the influence that the memory of her father had on the story. She reflects on the novel's protagonist, Jojo, who represents a masculine ideal often absent in her writing, and on the status of women's rights and protection in the rural environment.

NOT PROVOKED. OR WAS IT?

This book is perhaps the one exception to the observation I have made regarding my writing – it did not emerge from a position of anger or provocation. I willed it into being – wishing to see it appear.

Mother to Mother (1998) and *Beauty's Gift* (2008), its predecessors, were both definitely provoked. *Mother to Mother* was a response to an intimate tragedy: a killing in which two families were brought into close knowingness – the one of the other – by the awful incident. Because of a terrible murder, individuals who had not known one another become intricately involved in a horrific clash of feelings they had naught to do with, yanked into a soul-wrenching arena on opposing sides: victim and perpetrator. Both are shown to be sides of the same socio-political coin.

Beauty's Gift, the second novel, was provoked by the HIV and Aids pandemic, or, to be more precise, by how South Africans, as a nation, were dealing with the disaster – or rather, tragedy. It was a large-scale tragedy, for human lives were lost, some, if not most, unnecessarily. Had there been a better-informed leadership at the time, and thus a better-managed national programme, which was compassionate and worked from the heart, I sincerely believe most of those who succumbed might still be alive today.

It is commonly estimated that President Thabo Mbeki's HIV and Aids policies were responsible for more than 300 000 deaths. That staggering statistic reminded me (as if anyone could forget) of the tales of horror that had led to the publication of my book of poetry, *Please, Take Photographs* (2009). Words. Words. Words. Those words of poetry poured out of me, fired by the same anger as had previously provoked me into screaming words onto a page. The title of the collection is that of the poem which urges parents and caregivers to take pictures of children as a matter of urgency, since predictions for the youth of South Africa were that most would not reach the age of thirty.

But how did writing about HIV and Aids lead to writing my novel, *Chasing the Tails of My Father's Cattle* in 2015? Ah, cowardice! Or, to put it more generously, I wrote the book in response to criticism from readers – black male readers, to be precise. For even as praise was heaped on me and I was celebrated as an HIV and Aids activist for *Beauty's Gift* and *Please, Take Photographs*, published within a year of each other, a steady stream of criticism also hit me.

At almost every appearance I made in the wake of the book's publication, doing 'publicity' for the novel, at least one man in the audience would stand up and accuse me of hating black men. At times there would be more than one, from different corners of the hall, or an obvious group – three to six, more or less – would seem to have come for the sole purpose of challenging me and embarrassing me with their questions, which were not always relevant or significant or civil. Granted, a few were, but those were very few and far between. Foremost was the challenge, at times tentative: 'You seem not to like us very much?'

'Not to like you? And you being who, exactly? And why do you think that?'

My questions would bring loud, jeering laughter … But the long and short of it was that black men felt I had portrayed them in an unflattering manner.

I was not amused or, indeed, flattered by this attention. In truth, I was very scared. Believing I was meeting the challenge, helping to create an atmosphere of healthy dialogue which would eventually bring reason to bear, I learnt to ask: 'Well, help me out. Give me some lived examples of men who behave in ways so positively admirable, then I couldn't stop myself from portraying them in my next novel!'

Even as the silly words flew out of my mouth, memory painted dreadful pictures in my mind, in my heart. The dying I'd come to know all too well. The wailing at wakes, at funerals, and at sessions where a friend or relative shared their bitter pain, seeking comfort or, worse, financial assistance to help with medical treatment, even as the individual expressed fears it might already be too late – while to anyone with eyes, the terrible truth was clearly evident.

The situation was dire. But what maddened me as much as it saddened me was the plight of children. Of all the victims of the Aids pandemic, worst-hit were the children. What makes the plight of children excruciatingly worse than that of other victims of HIV and Aids is that children have absolutely no agency and are least able to prevent infection – having had no choice whatever in the behaviour that led to their predicament. If it angered me that 'faithfully married women are dying of Aids', as someone once said to me, you can imagine how furious I felt about the children, some of whom were born already infected – condemned to live a life of suffering, deprived of the good health most of us take for granted. Other children would grow up lacking parental love – both mother and father dead, victims of Aids. The luckier ones might be left with one parent who was disease free. But that was more the exception, very rare indeed. And poverty seemed to go hand-in-hand with illness. Medical attention costs lots of money, and many had no health insurance while many more were unemployed or had lost their jobs as a result of the very illness that now deprived them of the means to keep healthy.

Yes, HIV and Aids drove me to write a novel and a book of poetry. What motivated me was the horror of the children in that situation: girls (and sometimes boys, too) raped by 'minders'; children living with the awful knowledge of their vulnerability; the painful knowledge that there was no escape from their plight; perpetually aware that they were growing up defenceless, with no parental protection; certain of the fact that they would be raped, often repeatedly, by the same person or group of people, often acting in concert.

What kind of childhood was that?

That horror plunged me into my own childhood. I remembered the men I'd known and was grateful they had treated me and, as far as I know, other girls, with decency. Our childhood not violated, our spirits remained unsoiled; our bodies were respected and therefore protected. I remembered those young men, *oobhuti bethu*[1] we called them; even though they were not our real brothers, we referred to them as such out of respect. That is how we were raised. We did not call people older than us by name; in turn, they treated us as if we were their younger siblings. I will always be grateful for those *bhutis* of my youth, and I have remembered them in my writing. They are in one or two poems in *Please, Take Photographs* – thus, I have paid homage to them.

But where is *tata*[2] in your novels, I asked myself? Surely he was not the only father who was loving and caring and dutiful to his family? Where, indeed, were those men, the fathers of my childhood?

I remembered, and have never stopped marvelling, at how *Tata* was the father he was, even though his own father had not been there for him as a child. Abandoned while still in his mother's womb, *Tata* didn't set eyes on his father till age ten! His father – relatively educated for his times, and a clerk in the mines of Johannesburg – had 'died wearing a hat',[3] as far as his wife and son were concerned. But precisely because of the harshness of growing up fatherless, *Tata* must have vowed he would not put his own children through such misery. I say 'must have', for he never voiced that determination, that decision – though his actions shout it from the mountain tops. *Tata* Sigongo Penrose Magona was a good father. A very good father, and not only to his biological children but also to many more … relatives and, indeed, all the children who came into his orbit. Yet, as I have already stated, he was not the only adult male who was fatherly or big brotherly towards me and my playmates – as well as to the young women we became, forever leaving behind childhood, with its thrills and relative safety.

How come, then, I had not written *Tata* into my work? Could he not be a role model? Would that not be a fitting compliment not only to him but to all those *tatas* who had fathered me, including some I'd only encountered in passing. Grown men who would do for me whatever I needed done, for example in a situation of distress, having lost my train ticket, with no money in my pocket, they would give me what I needed, happy to discharge their duty in seeing a child safely home. But where are those men in my stories?

I had struggled with this question for some time. Even before retirement hit, I had attempted to write about *Tata*. For some strange reason, that attempt came out in poetry. Now, what publisher would publish a praise poem about a lowly 'Bantu' man who did not get himself arrested and tortured and jailed or hanged by the Boers? Sadly, none, and so that project fell by the wayside. But now, hounded by young men who felt misrepresented in my work, I went back to my attempt at representing *Tata* and others like him. Eventually, I took the conscious decision to write a novel in which the main character would be a man: loving and faithful to his spouse; gentle, if a little strict towards his children. A man who, despite the stern manner of his own parenting, would somehow manage to instil in his children the importance of being a protective and loving provider.

Jojo – the main character of *Chasing the Tails* – is, to a large extent, based on my father. The tragedy that befalls him at the beginning of the story stretches him as a character; by contrast, my father's life was mundane and rather uninteresting, and I was certain that no publisher would publish such a tale. Yes, he was a great father, but I couldn't see that unembellished life becoming the best-seller of the year. My character Jojo, based on *Tata*, turned out to be far from stern. And though he is firm, as when he takes his brother-in-law to court, he only does so when the traditional ways of settling domestic disputes have failed. I have been told by readers that Jojo is a most likeable man. I am quite happy with that perception, for, even though I stretched the truth in my creation of the character, in spirit, Jojo is Sigongo, my father.

Chasing the Tails of My Father's Cattle: the title itself is a metaphor. Through the life of this family – four brothers and their wives and children – through their ups and downs, their joys and upheavals, we see life as it was lived among my people in the villages of yesteryear: communal, with members of the village mutually supportive. Jojo's family lives in Sidwadweni, a village in the eastern Cape near Mthatha, where each individual is both valuable and valued, with each contributing to the well-being of the whole. Belongingness was a given – not taken for granted, but accepted and readily supported.

The 'tails' in the title are suggestive of something that is disappearing. Cattle, in the tradition of amaXhosa, stood for wealth or value – prized, admired and carefully tended. We see the face of a cow or bull when it is approaching, otherwise we see its tail. I chose the word 'chasing' to indicate that the person herding the cattle is running after the beasts, which are hastily being driven away by thieves.

Chasing the Tails of My Father's Cattle also suggests that the person is relatively young, or at least young enough to take care of his family's wealth. But that wealth is disappearing, hence the need to chase after it. Today, many things that are valuable to my people are also disappearing. S.E.K. Mqhayi[4] – famed philosopher, social commentator, historian, biographer – and unofficial poet laureate of the

Xhosa nation – has left vast traditional knowledge, which may arm not only amaXhosa, but black Africans in general against such loss. Anyone who has the heart, mind and soul to do so, can delve into and learn from Mqhayi's legacy to reclaim cherished practices from the past that can be put to use for the nation, and, indeed, the world. Mqhayi addresses the meaning and worth of tradition, and also alerts us to its vulnerability to time, and to the change that inevitably follows.

Among the topics he raises are wealth and how to handle it, as well as what we today describe as toxic masculinity. The latter brings to mind the story of a woman who became a respected mother of our nation, Albertina Sisulu, and the horrendous injustice and deprivation she and her family suffered after her father died. Ten-year old Albertina, the second of four children, was still in primary school, but her pregnant mother, a virtual invalid, was unable to assist with the money needed for her children's education. Though her husband had been a wealthy man, his cattle and fields were taken over by his brothers, leaving their late brother's children and their mother destitute. I recalled that story, blending it with Mqhayi's notion of tradition being vulnerable to changes wrought by the passage of time, and depicted this through the main character, Jojo, who shows that things change, indeed, should change, and that matters need not stay static during this process.

The story begins in rural Transkei in the pre-apartheid period, although in practice racially discriminatory attitudes and policies were already alive and well, even though apartheid had not yet been legalised. The story is replete with historic details, inter alia the Spanish flu, the working conditions of mineworkers, and race relations. However, the main thrust of this story is family life in a rural village in the late thirties to mid-forties in South Africa. Village life was at the time truly communal, and family life was close-knit, with a sense of togetherness – though this is not to say there were never disagreements or problems or calamities.

My story portrays an extended family of five brothers and their wives and children. The main character is Jojo. He and his wife, Miseka, plagued by child deaths, are childless. Where many men in that situation might find solace in the arms of other women who could give them children, Jojo remains loyal and loving to Miseka. The couple plans to give the latest child that Miseka is expecting the name Shumi or Shumikazi, depending on its gender. The name means 'the tenth' – for this is their tenth attempt. Despite the calamity of the past, the couple remains hopeful as they await this infant who, God willing, will be their only surviving child.

The man's huge love for his wife shines through, especially during the last stages of her pregnancy; the arrangements he makes so that he can be present at the birth of this long-awaited child, who follows on from the deaths of the previous nine, are remarkable. The couple has suffered miscarriages, stillbirths, infant and toddler deaths, and – worst of all – the two who actually made it to school and gave them hope, but also passed away.

The villagers are generally concerned and supportive. When they first realise that Miseka is again with child they wonder what name the couple will give that child. Jojo and his wife are running out of options – but so are the villagers. In those days, neighbours were mindful not to give their children a name either the same or similar to that of a neighbour's deceased child, as it would remind the grieving neighbour of their dead child each time they heard the neighbour's child being called. Community living was kind and generous and considerate.

Jojo is present when Miseka delivers her child. Her mother is also present, as is the local midwife. Even as labour pains start, prematurely, Miseka shows signs she is losing her own life. Jojo cries out like a wounded lion, despite his mother-in-law's admonition. Miseka hears the sweet sound of her baby's cry, and asks to hold her in her arms. She manages a soft kiss on the baby's head and says to her husband, *'Uz' ugcin' usana lwam!'*[5]

'Yes, I will!' grief-stricken Jojo promises. He feels absolutely bereft.

The rest of the story is about how Jojo fulfils that promise to his late wife. In carrying out his obligation, Jojo subverts many of his people's beliefs, their traditions – which are his own beliefs and traditions. Moreover, he subverts the accepted, expected life-long pointless working life of 'Bantu' men and does what is, to this day, little practised among not only black-black South Africans, but the majority of people throughout the world. Jojo takes mastery of his life: he not only plans but executes those plans.

Jojo is *Tata*, my father, not only as I'd known and experienced him, but as I dream him. As I wish him to have been. With the big heart he had, there is so much more he might have made of his life and of our lives, as his children, had he lived in a more just and generous time. With his work ethic and his dedicated concern for his family, including his extended family, I sometimes wonder what my father might have achieved, how he might have grabbed the opportunities available today, what equal pay for equal work might have enabled him to do, not only for his children but also for himself. But I also believe that the house of the past is better left behind, and so I plant my feet firmly in the house of today.

My dream, in the writing I do, is to open people's minds and hearts to the possibilities that elude them, the possibilities that are there … invisible, but there; obtainable with a little reach, a small stretch of imagination, a little urging, help, a pointer – whether accidental or through happenstance.

There for all.

I dream a better world – therefore, I write.

Even as I wrote this novel, with my father the model for Jojo, as the book unfolded, so did Jojo's being grow and expand. I realised that I myself had been 'fashioned' in the telling; that Jojo was all the fathers I had known, met, heard of; the men of my father's generation – men who saw all children as theirs to protect, shield, nurture and guide. I am very proud of what my father accomplished: staying married to our mother; working all his adult life; raising us, his children, and even, now and again, helping to raise the children of relatives. He was a good man. But Jojo, modelled after him, is a much bigger man, a great man. Fiction demands this kind of expansion – no insult intended to Sigongo Penrose Magona, none at all.

Through Jojo, I depict love as it is lived. Because of his love and loyalty to his wife, his love for his child, and his promise to dying Miseka, the mother of his only child, Jojo makes his daughter his only heir – something unheard of among amaXhosa, as patriarchy deems women not worthy of inheritance. Cattle, the pride of a home and family, should be kept within the man's family; this was the accepted assumption. When a young girl or woman married, her husband would automatically inherit what she had inherited. Yet that family wealth, which thus became the property of the husband's family, was never adequately compensated by lobola.[6]

A good work ethic ensures that Jojo not only keeps his job but gets raises, is given overtime work, and his wishes are accommodated. For example, he had wanted to be with his wife when the baby came in the February of the year Shumi was born and the bosses allowed him to go home for the birth then, rather than taking leave that December – that is, two months before the baby was due.

Jojo also demonstrates steadfastness in the face of vehement opposition from senior male members of his extended family when he decides, after his wife's death, to slaughter an ox as part of her funeral ritual. This was unheard of, as women are considered undeserving of such lofty consideration: a sheep or a goat would have sufficed – but Jojo stood firm!

Similarly, it is usually the preserve of grandparents to name a child, but Jojo sticks to the name he and Miseka had chosen – Shumikazi, or Shumi for short. Miseka's request – 'Please look after my baby' – is the fuel that drives Jojo: 'Daily, he vowed he would never go back on that promise. She was no longer on this earth, it was up to him, his duty, to do everything he could possibly do for their child.'

Widower Jojo raises his daughter, initially with help, but eventually by himself. As soon as he decided he would be a single parent, raising his daughter without his beloved wife, he planned for early retirement from the mines. Where he had been industrious before, he now doubled his efforts – working overtime, spending as little as possible of the little he earned; increasing his wealth by buying livestock and ensuring it is correctly reared. For example, he cut a deal no herdsman could refuse, giving the herdsman a portion of the herd he successfully reared. Not only did Jojo pay him well, he passed on the herding skills his own father had taught him. Consequently, by the time Shumikazi starts school, Jojo is in a position few African men ever manage to achieve – he voluntarily stops working for someone else.

His action astounds many who oppose and criticise him. When he stops working at the mines, many predict – telling him as much – that he will soon starve to death. Jojo proves them wrong. Back in the village, where he has come to stay, he removes his child from the care of his mother-in-law (Jojo himself having been long parentless). Now a permanent resident of the village, and no longer just on a three-week vacation from the mines, Jojo begins to notice things he had not seen while a regular mineworker. One such thing is that one of his sisters is in a terribly abusive marriage. People can pretend, put on a face, for a short period of time. However, with him being there permanently, that became nigh impossible for her. The truth will out, and it soon did in this situation. That brought me to another issue pertaining to tradition.

Finally, Jojo reimagines his relationship with his cattle. Traditionally, a man took pride in his herd; it marked him as a man of substance in a similar way to how Westerners regard wealth. But Jojo deliberately subverts the meaning and importance of cattle, as well as the associated traditions. Through Jojo, I show that there is more than one way to do things. The sentiment that practices can change is one that our ancestors voiced, which some, like Mqhayi, set down in writing. Mqhayi stated that tradition is, and should be seen as, time-dependent; it is neither God-given nor unchangeable. When circumstances change, it too must change.

To this day, among amaXhosa, indla-lifa[7] is always the firstborn male child – even when it is clear that he will not carry out the obligations of his role. Inheritance is not only about receiving the wealth left by one's predecessor. The role includes, inescapably so, the responsibility of taking care of all the dependents left behind. Included among those are the man's wife or wives, his daughters – married or unmarried or no longer married or widowed – as well as his sisters, whose lobola forms part of what his heir now inherits.

In the absence of a male heir, the closest male relative – usually a brother or uncle – is deemed the inheritor. However, against the bulwark of tradition, Jojo left his wealth to his only child, a daughter.

Most people, including amaXhosa and others in the southern African region who practise lobola have forgotten there is an associated practice: *ukutheleka*.[8] One of Jojo's sisters is in an abusive marriage, and she is regularly assaulted by her ne'er-do-well husband. Not only does Jojo *theleka* his sister, but he takes the man to court and gets justice for her. He does so even though many, including his brothers, oppose his actions and choose to support the man, even though they know he is abusive towards their own flesh and blood, their sister. Blood is thicker than water does not always hold when 'This is what men do' is key to a culture, with practices that have become so common that they are taken for granted and considered normal and nothing to write home about – never mind take issue with. Jojo, however, rescues his sister, not only from abuse, but also from a traditional practice that traps her in poverty.

He reminds amaXhosa, as well as others, of the other side of lobola – *ukutheleka*, which has conveniently been forgotten. Agency is also part of the path Jojo walks – not only for himself but, through family discussions, village meetings, and the example of his own life, for others too. Others witness the good that his actions result in. He is not only a nurturer but also a role model. Through *ukutheleka*, Jojo bodily saves his sister. Through the courts, he ensures that her errant, abusive, neglectful husband is not only punished but also made to pay reparations to his wife, whom he has physically maimed. And Jojo's helping her build a house of her own salvages her bruised self-esteem. However, even more significant is providing her the independence that is paramount for anyone seeking self-determination. She does not need a man – whether husband or lover – to ensure she has a roof over her head.

But Jojo is not admired by all. When he takes ill, and it soon becomes clear he will not long be of this world, many wonder what will become of his great wealth as he does not have an heir. Many, primarily his brothers, assume that they will be the beneficiaries. That made sense – but not to Jojo. He knows, and is aware of the unspoken expectations, just as he is aware of his fragile health. His wealth means gain to his brothers – the expectation of gain. Jojo sees the unfairness of it all. He sees how it all entails greed, as well as neglect – and the implicit unworthiness – of those born 'not male'. He is not willing to subject his beloved daughter to such disinheritance, albeit determined by tradition. And so, goaded by the voices of critics who accused me of hating black men, I was driven to re-membering men, black men who were good and kind and loving. My father leads this crew. However, I remember with great fondness and thankfulness, *oobhuti bam*, 'my older brothers' of Blouvlei location in Retreat, Cape Town. I am exceedingly grateful to them for the respect and kindness and love with which they treated me and other girls, my agemates, allowing us to have the childhood all children are meant to have – safe and secure from molestation.

Thank you, Tata. Without you, there would be nothing good for me to remember from my childhood, and this book would not have garnered the praise it has so far been fortunate to do. Thank you, S.E.K. – you helped me collect the cattle, showing that it is never too late to do the right thing. And since we can still see their tails, it is clearly not yet too late. We can still recoup what we have lost, what we are losing, and what we will continue to lose if we fail to act. We must act swiftly, boldly, and determinedly. Jojo, in this novel, is my father and all the men – young and not young, who were a wall of protection for little girls, young ladies, and women when I was growing up. Men who observed traditional boundaries, called out those who did not, and berated them for overstepping the mark. These are role models who left footprints, deserving to be represented in our work so that we may honour their example the world over, encouraging others, today's men – young and old – to follow in their footsteps.

God willing, and with the Ancestors nodding agreement, who knows, just around the corner, or in two shakes of a lamb's tail, perhaps … just perhaps … others will follow.

Listen. Just listen! I hear a shadow whisper: 'There is an awakening to your work … to the importance thereof'.

Chosi![9]

Zemk' iinkomo, magwalandini![10]

13.
WHY I WROTE *WHEN THE VILLAGE SLEEPS*

This previously unpublished essay identifies the catalyst for Sindiwe Magona's 2021 novel, When the Village Sleeps, *and provides the context that explains the significance of the title. It also provides a powerful example of Magona's willingness to advance a potentially unpopular position on sensitive issues – in this case, the efficacy of the government's Child Support Grant – to reframe highly polarised debates, and to offer compelling solutions for seemingly intractable problems.*

MY LATEST NOVEL, *When the Village Sleeps,* is perhaps different from anything that came before it. I began writing the novel with a clearer sense of purpose than usual as I was determined to speak to a problem related to our current moment in South Africa. I intended it to be a catalyst for change or, at the very least, to be at the forefront of change.

A writer, as with all living things, undergoes changes. This writer is no exception to this rule. I myself have changed, and continue to change. I am a very different person from what I was at the time of marrying, with no real thought to its ramifications – forced, really, into marriage by unplanned motherhood. That could not but be a frustrating experience; the children sure to be vulnerable throughout their childhood. Today, however, this writer is in a very different space – a position of mastery of my environment and also my life. Thus, I can begin to explain why I wrote *When the Village Sleeps* …

A few years back, I came across an article in my local neighbourhood newspaper, the *False Bay Echo*, which left me greatly disturbed.[1] The front-page article was prominently placed, so no one could fail to notice it. I certainly did not; I began to read the responses of a teenaged mother, who was interviewed by a social worker. It was a young mother's journey into motherhood. And there she was, pictured with baby on lap, smile on lips, looking proud as proud can be.

I wasn't long into reading it before I was struck by the central theme of the article with the young lady's responses: choice! As clear as clear can be, the young woman, a child, really, had planned each and every step of her way. Yes, at 16 she was holding a baby on her lap, her baby – and that was a choice. I read:

'I tried to get pregnant from when I was thirteen.'

Thirteen! My mind screamed. What was she thinking? Why? What made her want to get pregnant?

Of course, the last question was more reflex than rhetorical. It is what my brain registered, involuntarily, as it recoiled. When anyone wants to get pregnant, what they are really after is having a child. No one gets pregnant just for the fun of it; rather, it is the end result she is after. At 13, the mother being interviewed for this article already wanted a child.

Fine; I understand that at 13 a girl is probably outgrowing playing with dolls. But to *want* a child? Whatever for? What is she going to do with a child at such an early age, when she has not quite done being a child herself? And, is there nothing in between childhood with its fun-filled, carefree living and parenthood with all its attendant responsibilities? What about her education? It prepares the young for adult roles that loom when they reach that stage of development – the inescapable drudgery of adulthood. Education prepares the young for, among others things, becoming parents – responsible parents, I may add. And, God knows, our country, our nation, sorely needs responsible parents. Too many of our children, the nation's children, suffer from poor parenting, which appears in many guises, and with varying degrees of inadequacy. We have absenteeism, which may involve one or both parents; neglect, where, the child may lack the requisite material, emotional and spiritual support, including nurturing and guidance. In the latter case, the mere physical presence of an adult or adults does not automatically translate to anything approximating satisfactory parenting.

The article seemed to beg the question: why would someone that young saddle herself with the onerous responsibility of raising a child – and do so deliberately, actually plan an act of sheer recklessness? Moreover, how would she cater to the substantial needs of a child? Child-rearing is not for the financially ill-prepared, or for those who may lack other important features of responsible adult life, including intellectual, emotional and physical aspects. At 13, no one is ready – could be ready – for raising a child, never mind what the body may be telling her. Thank goodness the girl did not conceive when she first hatched the plan. If 16 is not an ideal age for starting a family, 13 is decidedly worse – for both mother as well as the baby.

Moreover, parenthood is crucial to nation building for, without robust, healthy and heartfelt parenting, there can be no healthy families. Without healthy, disciplined and thriving families, no nation can progress, never mind thrive! Why is she putting what amounts to a national resource at risk, jeopardising the future of the nation? The begetting of children by children is a calamity, and South Africa should stop accepting this as a norm – for the sake of the children and for the sake of the nation. We should not be so tolerant that millions of children are born daily into hopelessness and despair, thus increasing the poverty we daily decry.

But then, as I read further, there came a bombshell in the form of a confession, in the teenager's own words: 'I used to drink before I got pregnant'.

Clearly, this was someone who had been on the wrong journey for some time. Drinking alcohol is not usually associated with this age group. More often, we might hear this kind of statement – 'I used to drink' – from recovering alcoholics, or adults who are trying to give up a habit they no longer find satisfying.

She, all of 16 years old, 'used to drink' before she got pregnant.

'Please, God', I prayed, 'let her say she stopped once she'd got what she wanted. Let the fulfilment of her dreams give her not only satisfaction but care and concern for what she carries in her womb: the child she has wanted from such an early age.'

As a nation, we are fully aware we have a huge problem with foetal exposure to alcohol, which can cause physical, cognitive and behavioural problems. At present, South Africa is in the unenviable position of having the highest prevalence of Foetal Alcohol Spectrum Disorder (FASD) in the world. In 2005, the Western Cape province was found to have an incidence of 40.5–46.5 per 1 000 children compared to the 0.97 average in the developed world and a global average of 7.7.[2] This comes as no surprise when one remembers the sad fact of the 'dop system' that farmers used from colonial times and, I dare say, well into the present era. Labourers would be given alcohol in part payment for their labour. With Friday being the usual pay day, the weekend was broadly regarded as a time to get drunk. Many a child born to farm labourers would more likely than not show symptoms of FASD. This disorder is not new in our beloved country, though it is today more widespread and not uncommon even among professional people.

What followed in that newspaper article contradicted everything I had so long been praying for, regarding the country's youth. With shock, I read the girl's next words.

'I started drugs.'

Why? With this question still forming in my mind, the answer came, ferocious in its clarity.

'I wanted this baby to be deformed!'

Everyone knows that drugs increase the chance of birth defects leading to behavioural problems in early childhood and even more severe physical, emotional and cognitive defects. Yet, there it was, in cold naked black ink on the white page. The words of a mother stating a fact about her journey into motherhood: she had started taking drugs. She did that after she became pregnant – started taking drugs.

No, she did not stumble into drugs by accident. Again, her action was the result of choice. Just as choice had led her to pregnancy, choice led her to take drugs during the pregnancy.

The staggering admission forced me to read further. I needed to understand what was, to me, absolutely shocking: that the mother deliberately chose to maim her unborn. I asked myself, why? Why would anyone want to do something like that? With every atom in my body resisting, I read on. Forced myself to read further to perhaps understand the demonic deed.

The young mother-to-be had undertaken this act after an analysis of her situation. She had come to a deliberate and coldly calculated decision to maim the baby in her womb.

'My mother has three children. She does get the grant.[3] But she's always short of money. The grant's too little!'

So, the young lady had come to the conclusion: *not for me, such paltry offerings*. She would do better than her mother. There was a bigger grant available to children. Much better than the Child Support Grant (CSG)! But that grant was only for disabled children.

The Care Dependency Grant (CDG), given to children deemed 'severely disabled' today stands at R1 980 per child, per month. With a disabled baby, the girl would get 'almost ten times more than my mommy!' A quick check showed that, while she had exaggerated the difference between the two grants, the difference was still a significant one. Anything above a thousand rand a month is significant compared to less than half of that. But it goes without saying that nothing warrants putting in jeopardy the life of another human being.

I doubt anyone who read the article was not left alarmed, appalled, angry or worse. I know I was absolutely horrified. Where is her mother in all this? What kind of woman raises a child like this?

For days, the story would not leave me. The terrible deed done to the defenceless child in the young woman's womb was plain dreadful. That a human being might be born to never have a 'normal' life, and that through the callous act of the woman who had brought the child into being, was something my mind found hard to comprehend. Accept it, I could not. I could not accept that such things were taking place, and that we blithely continue with our lives as though nothing, absolutely nothing untoward was happening. Business as usual, in our beautiful, sunny South Africa.

But aren't the children of this nation *our* children, our community's children? Even our esteemed politicians say, often enough: 'Youth is the most precious resource of our nation!' With such proclamations, how does it happen that such an infant, still in its mother's womb – the most fragile state in the life of any creature – how does it happen that an innocent is subjected to so heinous an act such as the one perpetrated by the young mother? What is more, how is it that a mother does such a thing to the foetus in her womb, and the nation has no response for such an act? Why are there no repercussions? If, at any time, it might occur to me to take a pen and poke that pen into the eye of someone who happened to be in close proximity to me, I would need a very good lawyer and lots of money to avoid spending the night in jail. Why is this mother holding the baby she has maimed still free and not facing any legal action? This question seemed clear even from its absence in the article.

Now, please do not confuse this point with anti-abortion rhetoric. Here, I condemn harming a foetus that is brought to full term, for financial gain. This is an entirely different matter.

We are a country that becomes accustomed to things, even to the most nefarious of deeds. We get used to things we should not tolerate – the maiming of the not-yet born should affront the entire nation. It should be foremost among the things we refuse, as a nation, to countenance. But then, have we not, as a nation, lived with FASD for many decades? Why is the nation asleep, its eyes closed, with such a horrible thing staring us in the face – our collective face?

Something is amiss. No woman of child-bearing age should be unaware of the dangers of alcohol during pregnancy – to say nothing of illegal drug-taking. This should be part of the education of the young, for that is what education is all about, isn't it? Preparing the young for adult roles – for, of all the roles we play in adulthood, is any more important, more sacred, than the nurturing of the human race?

This is knowledge that our great-great-great grandmothers knew. Women of long ago knew this. Women who never knew the word 'school' knew that what they carried was new life; it was sacred, and they respected it. I remember how the women of my grandmother's generation, with their red blankets, people who could neither read nor write, nevertheless knew and respected their bodies, and held human life sacred. These women, who smoked *umbheka-phesheya*[4] and drank *umqombothi*[5] stopped both activities as soon as they knew they had conceived. 'Now I eat and drink for two people!' a woman would say, honouring and protecting the life she held 'under her ribs'. Long after I had read that newspaper article I was still fuming at this girl and her mother for their actions, but then I realised that it was the whole of 'Village South Africa' that needs to be lambasted for closing its eyes when such evils take place in plain view. My horror eventually turned to another terrible realisation: I was part of the problem … if only by the sin of omission.

S.E.K. Mqhayi stipulates communal responsibility in his 1914 work – which is also the first novel written in isiXhosa – *Ityala Lamawele (The Lawsuit of the Twins)*:

Ikwayindawo yomntu omdala ukuthi, nokuba usekhaya nokuba ungumhambi osendleleni, akhalimele, athethise, angxolise, ade ohlwaye, nawuphi na umntwana ambone esenza into engalungileyo. Yingozi kuye ukungathethi, kuba amehlo akhe, okanye iindlebe zakhe, se zimzele netyala.[6]

It is the duty of every adult to intervene whenever that adult comes across a young person doing what a human being should not do – whatever is out of the bounds of acceptable human behaviour. Even minor infringements would result in adult disapproval: '*Inkqayi ingena ngeentlontlo*'.[7] So, if a child or young person acted in ways the village did not approve of, they would be made aware that the conduct brought shame on their family. This was done to prevent socially unacceptable behaviour from spreading. But that was then, and now is decidedly a different time.

I realised that condemning the behaviour of the young woman would not change anything, and that condemning her mother would be worse, foolish even, and that condemning *all* of South Africa would be utterly useless. So I asked myself: what would be an appropriate action from me, an adult in this village – Village South Africa – to take in response to the article I had read?

I could not pretend ignorance and say, 'I had no idea what was happening' or 'I did not know such things were being done by young women'. But, having heard, what could or should I do? Where is my mountaintop, from whence I might sound the alarm? Surely the village, having heard it, would take action? But even if that were not the case, I could no longer sit and do nothing when innocents are at such terrible risk.

In outlining the idea I wished to propose, I drew encouragement from A.C. Jordan.[8] In his famed 1940 novel, *Ingqumbo Yeminyanya* (*The Wrath of the Ancestors*), Old Man Ngxabani asks of the court: 'Why, do you think, God still keeps me alive despite the *mpundulus*[9] of your womenfolk?' The character proceeds to answer his own question: 'For a reason. That reason being that I point out the way – point it out to the young – point it out for I have been there.'[10] By virtue of my seven decades and more of painful challenges and hard-earned knowledge, I decided that, like Ngxabani, I would address problems facing the country's youth, problems that were at the very heart of the government's child grant programme. But this would not be an indictment of the mothers who receive help in the form of grants.

It would be an indictment of the system – what it purports to do, and the chasm between its stated claims and what it in fact achieves. The grant system has conned people. For, were poverty alleviation actually taking place, the number of poor people in South Africa would not keep rising, year after year.

That poverty is growing in leaps and bounds is a well-known fact. For any with eyes to see, it is staring South Africans in the face. It stares at the faces of all who visit these shores. Shacks and hovels of all kinds dot the highways and byways of this land. In Cape Town, arriving by air, one's eyes are assaulted even before landing for, as the plane smoothly comes in to land, shacks in huge numbers seem to rise from the Cape Flats and the dunes to meet the descending aircraft. And then, all along the major arteries leading to the city centre, the scene is repeated with wearisome and worrying monotony. Poverty is South Africa, endemic and entrenched. We must not fool ourselves in thinking that the grant is achieving any poverty alleviation, unless by alleviation we mean 'prevents immediate death by starvation'.

No one can live on less than R500 per month. No one can live on R2000 per month. Not a baby, never mind a baby and its mother. But, despite that, most of the people receiving the grant are grateful for the money that has been coming to them for all of their 18 years. This, to me, is not a very optimistic programme. Eighteen years is the growing-up period in a life. By age 18, the baby on whose behalf the mother or carer receives the grant, is old enough to be a mother herself.

Do we really believe that, by this age, a young woman will be able to take proper care of her offspring? I rather doubt it. Thus, we have the perpetuation of poverty rather than its eradication. Indeed, I doubt it can even be claimed that we achieve alleviation.

The grant provides a mere minimum for survival; it does not encourage people to strive for anything better. And so, I took the opportunity to do what I could to discharge my duty to fellow humans who seem most in need of waking up to their own potential, their power, to effect change in their lives.

Personal growth or development can never be accidental, nor can it be bestowed upon one by another. It always involves active, persistent exertion by the individual concerned. Agrarian societies knew this very well: 'You reap what you sow'. The Bible says: 'You shall live by the sweat of your brow'. And post-apartheid South Africa says: '*Walala, wasala!*'[11]

I think back to my own lean years, my poverty-stricken young adulthood. At twenty-three, I became a single parent, mother to three children – all under the age of five. There was help available for vulnerable children – provided they were white or coloured or Indian. The apartheid government refused any form of social assistance for black children, Africans not recognised as citizens of their own country! I was forced to fend for myself and my children. It was only with the advent of democracy that social benefits for Africans became available, including the Child Support Grant. Today, I would have had the benefit of a CSG every month for each of my three children. What is more, I would have had that until each child reached the age of 18. I wonder what path my life would have taken if I had had the grant during those difficult years. Would I be better off than I am today? I doubt it very much.

I wonder, too, what the outcome of the grant is today – not only as regards the mothers who receive it on behalf of their children but, more importantly, for the children themselves. Is the modern woman who finds herself in a situation of penury better protected than her black sister of yesteryear? What, indeed, is this protection, and what does it mean for her and her child? When the woman depended entirely on herself, her family, her neighbours and her friends, what expectations and obligations were demanded of her? Does today's penurious woman owe similar obligations to the state? If so, what are these, and what do they mean for her and her child? I suspect that the answers to these questions are far from hopeful.

As a nation, South Africa needs to revisit the way it protects its most vulnerable – its children as well as the not-yet-born. This will of necessity entail an interrogation of the efficacy of grants, particularly the CSG, which is currently being strongly debated. Supporters of the CSG, including the government, maintain that it not only works, but helps children, youth and their caregivers enjoy a better life. On the other hand, responses of those who oppose it range from 'it encourages sponging' to 'girls get pregnant on purpose to get the grant', claiming also that the money is rarely used for the welfare of the children, the intended beneficiaries, and that, instead, the adults misuse the money on personal grooming, clothes, and even liquor. I am proposing a middle ground, whereby those in need are given assistance, but in the form of actual help that guides the recipients out of poverty.

The Social Assistance Act of 2004 obliges the state to provide assistance to vulnerable members of society. It is a pity, though, that the act does not incorporate any of the traditional ways of helping those who have fallen on hard times, for rarely, if ever, would a person who was experiencing a rough patch emerge from that situation without this having contributed in some way to their improvement. As the latter approach shows, real emancipation, including emancipation from hunger and disease, will always involve the active participation of the person who wishes to rise and become what they are meant to be.

Traditionally, the poor were assisted, but they were helped in such a way that they stopped being poor. A marked difference between the traditional way of helping the poor and current methods is that the poor were required to be part of the solution. *Inqoma* is one such traditional method: when someone loans a cow so that the borrower can have milk for his children, which entails caring for the beast that is on loan. All being well, the cow will calf and the herd will grow in number. Once there has been a significant increase in the herd, the cow's original owner, who had facilitated *inqoma*, claims his share of the beasts. However, the loan binds the person being helped out to properly care for the beast he has been loaned. Should it not be treated in a fitting manner, the owner would be quick to reclaim his possession, his wealth. The man receiving assistance has to practise proper animal husbandry or lose out on the loan.

In the case of agriculture, the same principle applies. When one has finished ploughing one's own fields, one clubs together with a few others to organise a span of oxen; on an appointed day, the group presents itself at the home of a neighbour who, for some reason, is not in a position to plough his own field. His neighbours bring their own cattle, implements and seed. But, if the neighbour does not do the work he is meant to do – watering, pruning, etc. – and the crop fails, he will not get anyone's help if he needs it the next season. The village helps those who help themselves; it does not encourage avoiding one's responsibility.

The fact that the social grant system encourages no active participation on the part of the grantees would be regarded as infantilisation by traditional society. The South African Social Security Agency (SASSA)[12] should include an educational aspect that is part and parcel of the actual grant. Thus, young people receiving grants might receive skills training or, if academically inclined, they could be assisted with furthering their education; the aim should always be to enable people to stand on their own two feet. Self-sufficiency should be the ultimate goal. Government, therefore, ought to be encouraging and enabling young people to work toward this end. Of course, this would require an adjustment of the system, involving much effort and creativity, so that all of society can look forward to a real shrinking of poverty as more and more recipients work towards graduating out of the system and into genuine independence.

The unfortunate circumstances surrounding the social grant indicate that the transition from apartheid to democracy is far from complete. For black women living under apartheid, social assistance was totally absent, as was the vote. Today, there is confusion around these things, with many declaring: 'At least this government is doing something for us!' Many view the social grant as a right previously denied them. Lost is the purpose, the true purpose of the grant: to tide one over a rough patch. It should not be used to subsidise a lifestyle! People should be helped out of poverty, not condemned to dependency during their early years, which merely entrenches poverty.

I have expressed my disgruntlement with the grant and offered ideas for its improvement primarily on behalf of the person who is most damaged by the present situation – the child who comes into the world less than whole because of its mother's actions. Troubling questions arise when considering this crisis from the children's perspective. How do they feel when they come to the devastating realisation of what has happened? That they will be forever disabled, physically and/or mentally, because of the deliberate act of their mother? What recourse is there for such a child?

The pathos of the teenage mother's child was magnified, for me, in two devastating details in the story's closing. Firstly, the article stated that the story represents 'a growing trend'. And, secondly, the mother – pictured smiling, as though she had not a care in the world – admitted, 'Sometimes, when I see she will never be like the other children, I'm a little sad', adding, perhaps by way of consolation, 'But I love my *gogga*[13]!'

14.
WHY I WRITE CHILDREN'S STORIES

In this previously unpublished essay, Sindiwe Magona explains her motivations for writing children's literature (becoming one of the most prolific of such writers in Africa) and her understanding of the uniqueness of the genre. Her decision to write stories for young readers, the essay suggests, is linked to her deep conviction that South Africa's youth need to be protected and nurtured if they are to become responsible citizens of the country.

IT WOULD BE wonderful if every child had a carefree, fun-filled childhood. I know this, because I did. Day was a time for playing games, climbing trees, roaming hills and valleys, and hunting for edible roots and berries. And when sun went to her mother and our mothers called us home as the stars started popping out to twinkle and wink up in the sky, we ran home. Gleefully, we ran home to grandma – not mama. Mama called us in – called us home. But, in our hearts and minds, without any doubt, we knew she only called us to go to grandma, and that it was she to whom we were running. Grandma didn't have to invite us. We knew she was sitting there, the bright-burning fire before her, waiting for us. Yes, the fire and grandma waited for us as mama called us back home. So we ran back home and joined *makhulu*,[1] making a semi-circle around the fire with its three-legged pot. Our mouths watering, the smell of whatever was cooking in that pot making us salivate, our eyes glued to the majestic figure huddled with back slightly bent, stout, strong, ready ... then, as soon as we were settled, quiet, our ears pulled us to the words pouring out of *makhulu*'s mouth:

'*Kwathi ke kaloku ngantsomi* ...'[2]

At once, all thought of food flew from our minds as we wandered far away ... seeing what *makhulu* painted in such vivid manner, her voice rising to the sky, chasing the moon, or falling so-so-so soft and faint, as a child hears the stalking beast ... stealthy ... slow ... ever so slowly coming closer, getting ready to –

Today, I tell stories. Write stories. I doubt I would do so had I not had the childhood I'd enjoyed. A childhood where storytelling ended the day, sending the child to bed happy, tired and satisfied, her imagination fired up by impossible adventures while sitting around the evening fire, *makhulu* taking her on a trip to lands far, far away ... impossible to forget. Worlds filling her mind, her spirit, her whole being, with the magic that is life ... so that, when she herself became *makhulu*, she would claim:

I am a writer. *Makhulu* as well as other adults of my childhood and, later still, books that came into my hands, gave me that gift – planted, watered, and grew it in me. And so I write; I am called a writer.

I am also a storyteller, and I tell my stories in two languages: isiXhosa and English, my two working languages. I write children's books in both these languages; each story may start in either of the two. That is to say, when I first conceive of a story, it comes as a story that usually wants to be written in the one or the other language. I think that this, primarily, has to do with what accompanies the conception of the story – what moves or prompts me to write it. If that prompt suggests, or seems to suggest, a national audience, then the story, most probably, will be in English – although, most certainly, I will then proceed immediately to translate it into isiXhosa. On the other hand, if the story arises from a situation or idea about the African child in a township or village, then the story will first be crafted in isiXhosa, since it will be directed at, or speak to, the child whose mother tongue that is. That story will need the palette, idiom and other specificities with which that child is familiar.

Writing is sharing, and there is nothing better to share, especially with children, than the sheer joy of diving into a story and telling what happened, a long, very long time ago, in a place far, far away, to someone or something very, very different to, or just like you!

The magic of the Story World is indescribable.

I remember the joy of listening to good stories. I remember the wealth that they brought me, the vivid characters, some that I would never forget, and their deeds of courage, of deceit and deviousness, of cruelty and of kindness without compare. I remember how I often identified with, or wished for, such and such a characteristic or trait. Wanted and hoped with all my heart that a particular outcome would prevail, and, sometimes it did, but more often than not, things didn't work out the way I had hoped. And I learnt, without being aware I was doing so, of the unpredictability of life. And there was always another story ... and another ... and another. Sooner or later, things would get better, and certain characters reappeared. Where there was sadness, laughter came ... and I learnt, again without knowing I was learning, that, although there may be problems, there were solutions too and, eventually, things worked out ... sometimes very well, indeed. That optimism is invaluable in this unpredictable life.

All through my life, I have been fully aware that the choices I make are the result of stories I have had the privilege of drinking in, or characters I have admired whose journeys have, in some or other way, touched me. Indeed, although not often, I have paused to wonder how such a character might have reacted, what they would have done if confronted with my situation at the time. What a particular character might think of me for the choice I was considering.

This is what I hope I convey to my young and not-so-young readers. The sense of wonder, of awe, of discovery – and the ability to identify with children from elsewhere, in terms of time or space or culture or whatever else, in the stories I write.

I write stories about *us* – about the people, places, spaces and events of South Africa – but I also write stories about people from elsewhere. After all, elsewhere may be just like home in many, many ways. And that is why I write children's books about general, everyday things – siblings, parents, friends, bullies, parties, tragedies, special days, special people, special pets and other animals – all of which are hugely exciting to young minds and hearts. We should never forget that, as much as children may already know things, they are also, all the time, busy learning new things about the world around them as they see life daily unfold and expand before their awe-filled eyes. That is the sense of magic which reading can bring to children – the continuous discovery of the sheer marvel that is life.

The first day of school, the first day at big school, learning to read, learning to write, learning to walk or talk or swim, doing something bad, like taking money out of mommy's purse, or doing something good, like returning the neighbour's cellphone you found outside his yard: I write to remind children of each of their milestones, and the joy they experienced. Think of what it means to come into this whole wide world – brand new. The newness of it all, which we soon forget, the infant being a brand-new person. The world is new to a baby – everything about it waiting to be experienced, to become acquainted with, to be identified and classified – deciding what is good or bad, what you like or dislike, what you want and don't want ... wow, how wonderful!

That is what I write about, and that is why I write for children. Adult books are about angst. Children's books are about wow! And, yes, there may be some, very little, angst ... but it is usually delicious, even delightful angst – soon to be overcome and even embraced – growth-related angst. Even the evil of witches has a purpose, unlike the senseless brutality we find in much adult literature – the more gore, the larger the audience and the bigger the sales. Children's bestsellers are about the wondrous world all around us. They convey – or should convey – our relatedness to that, show us or make us feel we are part of that wondrous world, that we belong to it and it belongs to us, for together we make up the world. Books, especially children's books, should help us understand that we must cherish ourselves and cherish all of life too. Everything on this earth is here for a reason, and ours is to stay alive and alive to the responsibility that is ours, which is to help the earth to live and continue living.

That sense of belonging is crucial. Every child should grow up filled with the certainty that they are an essential part of the world, and though the world is a very big place, each and everyone and everything in it has a place and is no more or less important than any other. Each of us has a role to play. Without you or me – without the ant or the elephant – the world would not be complete. Children should grow up with the intrinsic knowledge that they have a reason for being. Just as children learn that flowers bloom and some trees produce fruit, each child should wonder: What is *my* fruit, my reason for being? What can I do with this precious gift that is my life?

I write books in their mother tongue so that children whose language is isiXhosa can enjoy the story without struggling with language. For language is there to help us understand, to communicate. Our children shouldn't be handicapped even before they get to the content of the story. Can there be any fun when understanding is hampered, when half the story contains words and nuances that are a mystery to the young reader?

There is a growing belief that a baby can 'hear' stories even in utero, for science confirms that they can hear language – the mother tongue – a truth that the Ancients must surely have intuited. Babies should be read to, hearing not only words but also expressions, picking up on idioms, taboos – things which contain a wealth of cultural information that the child drinks in with the effortless ease of breathing in life-giving air.

While all stories enrich, mother-tongue stories do a whole lot more; they anchor the child into the specific realm of one's deepest, essential self, which is inalienable and eternal. Just as no child should ever be denied the citizenship of the country of their birth, no child should be denied the privilege of the mother tongue. It is a birthright, sacred. To de-tongue a child, whether by neglect or design, should be considered a criminal act.

Children who read or hear stories in the mother tongue are much more likely to meet themselves in books, to see, hear and learn from characters who remind them of themselves, in familiar situations, and with similar problems. Even the ring of the 'new' in the story will be seen as something possible within their world, it will not be entirely 'otherworld'. Thus, young imaginations are fired!

Lively, interesting books – new ones as well as old favourites – should be introduced to children throughout the country. That would mean translation into all the other languages of the country – while there are 11 official languages, there are many more than this. We could then raise children who would have access to books across the spectrum of languages, and the possibility of growing into adulthood with a shared memory of stories from their childhood. In the same way as children in other cultures have a shared knowledge of the Pied Piper of Hamelin or Hansel and Gretel, South African children should be able to recognise tales from their own storytelling traditions. It is something of a crime that there are people who emerge from high school with no knowledge of the works of Nadine Gordimer and J.M. Coetzee, South Africa's own literature laureates, and no knowledge whatsoever of African classics written in indigenous languages, such as *Ingqumbo Yeminyanya* (*The Wrath of the Ancestors*) or *Ityala Lamawele* (*The Lawsuit of the Twins*), most of which have since been translated into English and are therefore widely available.

Stories are an integral part of a child's socialisation. They are also fun. However, stories also teach us important things, for example, even though danger or evil or hardship may come our way, eventually, after some struggle, good may prevail, with order restored. It is important that children grow up with a sense that order generally prevails in the world; that, despite life's hardships, most human beings are equipped with an inherent strength to overcome calamity, and to triumph.

Such lessons were a central component of *iintsomi zesiXhosa*, the folktales of amaXhosa. My childhood was nothing if not magical: the evening's inevitable story time eagerly looked forward to by us all. Grandmothers were the storytellers of my childhood although other grownups, female and male, would also tell *iintsomi* to us of an evening. Folktales, I firmly believe, were used by our forebears, long before reading and writing came to these parts, as an integral part of the socialisation of the child. The child would be transported to other realms, which is the magic of stories and storytelling, with imagination playing a big role. Through the descriptions she hears, the child 'sees' different things: animals big and small; flying creatures that make different sounds; lands far, far away ... different yet somehow similar because of shared emotions, hopes, dreams and fears, as well as adventures known and unknown, all quite magical!

Human beings the world over share the same emotions: love, hate, courage, cowardice, anger, honesty, dishonesty and so on. But what are the many faces of each of these? How do children experience and express them? Are there appropriate and inappropriate ways of expressing a particular emotion? Through stories, children see others express dismay, disappointment and anger. They see what happens in each case, and what the consequences are. In a country such as South Africa, where our beautiful diversity means different ways of doing the same 'right' thing, it is important that children learn the full meaning of that diversity, that they learn about acceptance and tolerance.

Stories are the beautiful dreams of our world about itself, in all its multiplicity. They are the surest way of demonstrating what it is like to be a human being, in such and such a society, and at such and such a time. Whatever age we happen to be, we are *all* the stories we tell – and all of us are the stories we hear, that we listen to, and which we enjoy.

That is why, in our wonderful country, South Africa, I write for all our children – the children of the nation, future grownups upon whose shoulders sits the health and well-being of an entire nation that is yet to come into being. Most importantly, all children everywhere need to hear stories of who they are, and what that means. Perhaps, even more than children elsewhere, the children of South Africa need stories that knit them together, help them find commonality, remind them that they are kin. Our children need stories that can help them not only to bear or survive the burden of our past, but also to successfully negotiate the journey that is theirs to follow, so that they can transcend the country's hideous past, a past that has bequeathed us all an unenviable, unbearable woundedness. Interesting stories with characters that the children of this country can relate to, facing problems with which they themselves daily contend, are needed as a matter of urgency. The acculturation we have all undergone needs mending; we need deculturation and re-culturation and intra-culturation. Children's stories, new fairytales and folktales are needed, showing characters confronting cultural differences in creative ways, which could lead to eyes being opened so that there is understanding rather than rejection. This might perhaps even lead to admiration, with the incorporation and embrace of what was previously seen as different and even alien. We see this with our songs, our dances, and even in the way we dress – so why not with story too?

The latest of my children's books, *Skin We Are In*[3], is precisely such a book. It is not only for the children of South Africa but for children – and grownups – everywhere. It is a book I did not 'dream' but was invited to co-author by world-renowned American anthropologist and palaeobiologist Nina Jablonsky, a fellow of the Stellenbosch University Institute for Advanced Studies (STIAS).[4] This institutional support is indicative of the importance of the topic in relation to the children of South Africa. In addition, an Afrikaans-speaking donor provided substantial funding, which enabled publication at an affordable rate, thereby making the book accessible to many who could not otherwise afford it. Our children need to grow up confident in the knowledge that skin colour should be no determinant in life, aware that it holds no significance or value with regard to the individual wearing it.

Coming from our history in South Africa, this is a leap into the Valley of Happy Colour-Free Attitudes (free, that is, from prejudice linked to skin colour). The story of Njabulo and his classmates is one of discovery, of truth and the personal growth that comes from this. That is the power of story. And, it is in pursuit of such truth – for myself as well as for the young readers who honour me by reading my books – that I write books for children. *Skin We Are In* is, in my humble opinion, perhaps best suited of all my books to instil this sense of the oneness of humanity. The latter is a not unimportant ideal; it is, indeed, the essence of our nationhood. The true meaning of our Rainbow Nation – multiculturalism, peaceful coexistence, acceptance of ourselves and one another, as we have been created – this, in a nutshell, is the essence of *Skin We Are In*.

Storytelling, on a regular basis, is our best hope, not only for children but also for families, to nurture a new spirit of mutual understanding and tolerance, if not, as yet, mutual appreciation. Rather than being monochrome and monolingual, family storytelling groups should, as far as possible, be reflective of our country's diversity; we all have something to learn from each other, whatever income level we belong to. In other words, we are all opportunities for mutual enrichment of the South African soul, which could lead to our common goal: peaceful coexistence. This is at the centre of human existence, for without that essential ingredient, humanity would perish. Hence, among other ways of ensuring our continued existence, the international community has institutionalised human rights. And, because of the particular fragility and vulnerability of children, we also have – above and beyond these human rights – the United Nations Charter of Children's Rights. These include Article 31, which ensures 'the right of the child to participate freely in cultural life and the arts' and 'to participate fully in cultural and artistic life'.

Where better to start planting the seed than in childhood – and the earlier, the better. I was fortunate to see this in practice when I participated in the 2022 Mandela Day celebrations held at the Centre for Early Childhood Development in Lansdowne, Cape Town; the large number of children that attended the Centre had reaffirmed my belief that children really matter at that place. At the climax of the evening, a book was launched: *Madiba: Our Children's Champion*, comprising a collection of Nelson Mandela's speeches about children.[5]

The book is brilliant; the first half is comprised of words that Madiba[6] himself spoke about children. Every image of Madiba in the book was created by a child – whether drawings, sketches or paintings – and there is no mistaking his well-known face. The children had captured the essence of the legend, South Africa's iconic 'Children's Champion'.

The whole world is aware of the deprivations Nelson Mandela suffered while on Robben Island and, later, Pollsmoor Prison, infamous places where he was incarcerated for over a quarter of his life. Because of its geographical setting – Robben Island was a maximum-security prison on an island – and because he was often in solitary confinement, Mandela was often lonely, and he also experienced deep sadness. As he said in an interview at the United Nations Headquarters during his first visit to the United States, one of his most painful memories of Robben Island was the absence of young life. He sorely missed the cry of a new-born baby, children's chatter, and the patter of tiny feet. It is clear that he held children very dearly in his heart: 'South Africa's children shall play in the open veldt, no longer tortured by hunger or disease or threatened with abuse. Children are our greatest treasure';[7] and 'There can be no keener revelation of a society's soul than the way in which it treats its children'.[8]

Mandela must surely be turning in his grave because of how Village South Africa not only neglects its children, but also ill-treats them, abuses them, kills them, rapes them … My most recent novel, *When the Village Sleeps* (2021), a book for grownups, was provoked by the deliberate maiming of babies in the wombs of their mothers – the very people who ought to be their protectors. While this book was not written for children, it is my love of children that led to my writing it. I hope and pray my book does the work of opening our eyes as Village South Africa, that it stirs us to action aimed at ending evil practices, thereby saving children who are yet to be born. And so, while I could be said to write for and also about children, I in fact write to ensure their safety and well-being, to make sure that they experience joy – and thrive!

CONCLUSION
A TRIBUTE TO THOSE WHO CAME
BEFORE ME

This essay begins with the speech that Sindiwe Magona delivered at the Franschhoek Literary Festival in 2015 in honour of André Brink, whom she considers a literary ancestor. She follows this up with a reflection on the diverse voices that have shaped her as a writer.

I FEEL HIGHLY honoured by the Franschhoek Literary Festival[1] and the Brink family, especially Karina Magdalena Brink, André's widow,[2] for inviting me to participate in this year's festival.

First, let me share with you how I arrived at the title of my talk, 'Andre Brink: Enigma, Betrayer, Villain or Hero: An Outsider's Take on this Giant of South African Letters'. This is my personal reflection on who I am next to André Brink; when, where and how our paths crossed; and what those encounters meant, as well as what they have come to mean to me.

No doubt, you – or at any rate, many of you – will agree with me that I am an outsider in this situation, an outsider looking in at the particular life of one André Phillipus Brink. I am an outsider because of who we were not so long ago when there was no way I could have been anything but an outsider in the life of this man. However, our paths did eventually cross, some 25 years ago, in 1990, to be precise, when something I would never have dreamt of happened: I became a writer. Anywhere else in the world, this would not be a noteworthy event. But given who I was – the where and the when – it was indeed remarkable.

Shortly after my first book was published in 1990, I was invited to my very first writer's conference, at the University of Cape Town. UCT was a foreign country to the likes of me. Brink could have studied there. He in fact lectured there. But it was forbidden territory to one such as I. However, this was different. I was not going there to study or lecture, but to a one-day affair – a writers' conference. So, I travelled, all the way from New York to Cape Town to a conference of people who wrote, and called what they did 'work'!

It was at the same conference that some learned person who had studied such things (things most of us know, but in a vague, unformed way) said that, since the first African woman was published a century or so back, only five South African women had achieved the status of writer. He said this in 1990! I, for one, had come a very, very long way with my humble offering that same year – my first autobiography, *To My Children's Children* (1990).

It was that one event that brought me within shouting distance of André's life. Had I not begun writing and, by a strange turn of events, found a home in the prestigious company that also published his works – David Philip Publishers – I doubt very much I would ever have come to know André Brink, never mind call him a friend.

However, I don't think I actually met André that year of the conference, the year my first book was published. He was probably out of the country – something he seemed to do as naturally as the rest of us breathe in and out. France seemingly was one of his more favoured destinations.

It was in fact with the publication of my first novel that we would meet and sit at the same table, over a meal, at the house of our publishers – David and Marie Philip – in Claremont.[3] You cannot imagine how nervous I was.

The mere thought that I would meet him, be in the same room, sit at the same table, and be expected to be in conversation with him – oh, the thought filled me with dread!

I'd come to writing rather late, and thus, it was with all the reverence and awe of a novice or acolyte that I approached the High Priest. I attribute this to the fact that, unlike many emerging writers today, I was not in my teens when my first book came out. I have certainly not suffered an excess of novices stuttering and stammering merely by being in close proximity to me. But then, again, I have yet to achieve a stature which may warrant such adulation. I can assure you, stutter and stammer I certainly did when I met The Great André Brink, for the very first time!

I had every intention of showing due respect – genuflecting and everything else I thought necessary. But when the man himself walked into the room, immediately recognising him from pictures I had seen on the covers of books and in magazine articles, all I could think was Lord above ... he is tall! Yet even then – long before age shrank me – even then, everybody was tall compared to me. It took me a long time, well into middle age, before I came to link the imposing height of others with the absence of same in yours truly!

André Brink was not only tall, but elegantly dressed in an understated way, with nothing screaming DESIGNER! Instead, a subtle, intangible yet insistent, indefinable something whispered 'GQ' (Good Quality)! The man had presence. He walked into a room, and all talk stopped. But he had a wicked sense of humour and there was never a dull moment ... once you got to know him.

However, from the word go, seemingly without effort, André somehow managed to calm me down, making me not only completely at ease around him but also delighted to be in his company.

Those who know me – who *really* know me – know that I am painfully shy. Therefore, to get me not only relaxed but enjoying the company ... that took some doing. Or should have – but, as I have said, it just happened – just like that.

As I got to know André over the years, I do not recall ever exchanging anything other than enjoyable, enriching, inspiring, challenging words and ideas; not once did we have a disagreement (and those who know me will tell you that is nothing short of a miracle). That was André's gift. He was empathetic, understanding, charming, and, over time, I came to see that we had something in common other than our writing. There was a streak of shyness there. I may be wrong, of course, but to me, André was a little shy. What a delight to discover that! Clearly, it takes like to recognise like.

Mother to Mother (1998), my first novel, is a book he endorsed with a blurb that made me feel better even than if I had won the Lotto. He said it was a *classic*! If he were around today, he would be saying, 'I told you so!' Last year, 20 years after André Brink had called the novel a classic, the Department of Education prescribed it for Grade 10 mother tongue or first language.

Such support from an established, indeed very well-established author, is invaluable to an emerging author. André understood this, and was generous in his affirmation of those coming up behind him, chasing him and perhaps even threatening to unseat him. For that is what writing is: a competition, with each successive generation of writers wanting to unseat the preceding generation ... *c'est la vie, n'est-ce pas?*[4]

And that is the enigma that was André Brink – for me, a Big-Man Name with no airs whatsoever – indeed, he was almost humble. For a beginner like myself, it was incomprehensible that such an important writer (male and white!), whom I had expected to be completely unapproachable, could offer such a warm presence.

Brink was one of the leading figures of the movement that came to be known as the Sestigers[5] – writers who had significantly broadened Afrikaans literature. This was not received with applause by the Afrikaner establishment. As might be expected, neither the government nor its supporters were amused by these upstarts, whose work precipitated a cultural collision of mammoth proportions. Afrikanerdom saw the movement as an assault on all it stood for, labelling these writers traitors. It felt they had betrayed their nation.

What the Sestigers had done was to break loose of the *laager* – as Afrikaner insularity is often described.

The Sestiger writers, who included luminaries like Breyten Breytenbach, were Afrikaners by birth, and chose to write in Afrikaans, but their writing set them apart. They followed a new truth – their own truth. And that was not easy. It was not easy then, and it is not easy now. Indeed, it never will be easy. This group of writers was perceived as betraying the cause of Afrikanerdom, an important element of which was building the language, Afrikaans. They were also, of course, considered villains. But the Sestigers believed that the political context within which their work was located could not be ignored. The vast numbers of people who were part of their land – and their lives – could not be kept out, invisible in their work.

In the context of South Africa, exactly who – or what – is a villain is not always clear. This is certainly true of our not-so-distant past, when it was not always obvious who was a villain and who a hero; indeed, a man or a woman might be labelled both, depending on who was doing the labelling.

To explain what this would mean for André Brink, I will take the liberty of telling a friend's story. At the time, I did not yet know this friend, who made headlines in all the newspapers in the country – as well as overseas. He held a lofty rank, perhaps an admiral, in the South African Navy. But he was a spy! For the Soviets and for the African National Congress.

While I didn't yet know the man himself, I did know that the headlines in the Afrikaner papers screamed his name, and his foul deed. For what he'd done was a foul deed in the eyes of the regime, but it was music to the ears of all the oppressed peoples of South Africa. Finally, there was a crack in the armour of apartheid! Finally, one of them had seen the evil of the system: a ray of hope was given to people who neither knew, and would probably never know, this man. Still, to them he was a hero. In the literary community of the world, André Brink was just that kind of hero.

I have been looking back at the journey I have walked, by some strange stroke of luck, at certain interesting moments, with André Phillipus Brink.

He is someone I could, and did, call a friend, and from whom I drew tremendous courage to go on going on, living my life mindful of what it was I was doing with my pen. He was a hard act to follow, but that's the way things are. *Inyathi ibuzwa kwabaphambili!*[6] Traditionally, hunters ask those ahead of them what direction the quarry has taken; the information is handed on to those who follow behind – in this case, those who pursue the craft of writing.

There are not many white-male South Africans whose passing I have mourned. But with André Brink, I was not merely saddened when he left us; I mourned his passing. I grieved, and miss him still. When the then Dean of Humanities at the University of the Western Cape called me at Georgia State University in the United States to give me the sad news, my reaction was short and simple: *Kuwe umthi omkhulu.*[7]

Once more, thank you very much, Karina, my friend, for the honour you and the Franschhoek Literary Festival have bestowed on me by giving me this opportunity to pay my respects to my friend André and to honour his memory. I thank you, all.

This speech was a first for me. The first time I had publicly applauded a writer, and such a writer, too. A man. A white man. That was crossing many, many borders – a very good sign for who we as a nation were becoming. The occasion grew me, for it affirmed me as a writer. However, thinking back on it, I realise I have long been singing the praises of other writers – if not publicly – including those who left their wordmarks indelibly on my mind, even though those were never in print, never published, never acknowledged as 'literature'. For what is writing but the conveyance of thought through the medium of the written word? I have known not a few such luminaries whose thoughts will stay with me till the day I die, despite those thoughts never having made it through the narrow gates of a publisher.

It is these people, and many not mentioned here, whom I wish to applaud – the publicly acknowledged writers as well others who are equally important in the making of this one writer. I pay tribute to them all and declare that, to a large extent, I am their progeny; I write because they wrote. I am not necessarily doing something new or better, though there is always the hope that there may be some degree of significance, some kind of illumination. Whatever the case, I hereby doff my hat to my forebears – my s/heroes.

I had enjoyed reading as a child and later, too, as a teenager. I was lucky enough to have books given to me by a neighbour, and to have access to the Langa High School library, which, for all its limitations, served me very well at the time. It was there that I fell in love with the Hardy Boys, the popular American mystery series. And I did not escape the classics: Shakespeare, E.M. Forster, the Brontë sisters (I loved *Jane Eyre!*), and George Eliot – whom no teacher of mine ever revealed was not a man. And then there was James Joyce's *A Portrait of an Artist as a Young Man*. Yes, these books fed my own story, as I delighted in what I read. However, I did not see myself producing anything remotely resembling these – for who wrote books like this and looked like me?

In terms of writing that I could relate to personally, my gratitude goes first and foremost to black women writers – South African, African, and those in the African diaspora – who gave me the feet I needed to walk in undertaking this writing journey. When I first began to imagine my future, I needed to see people who looked like me, who were recognised as writers. White writers of any gender could not do that for me. Their writings were preoccupied with – and sometimes deeply conflicted over – their inherited position of superiority. The situation was similarly inappropriate when it came to black male writers. Theirs was not a story I could echo.

So, it was black women writers who birthed the writer that I am today. Even with that group, however, there was work to do before I could get to a point of identifying with any of them, as in: 'Ah, there's someone just like me doing this … so maybe I can, too!' Part of the blame for this absence of ready identification with my own kind falls on the shoulders of teachers, their inattentiveness to the socio-historical aspects of literature – to say nothing of the psychological. How much earlier I might have picked up a pen if a teacher had noticed my inclinations and steered me in the right direction!

Minazana Dana is the only female writer I can recall from my primary school days. She wrote *Kufundwa Ngamava* and other classics in isiXhosa that were on the syllabus in African schools during apartheid. That name got embedded in my brain precisely because it was a woman's name – a very rare occurrence. Before that, I had never seen a book written by *umXhosakazi*[8] or, for that matter, any woman of colour. It says a lot about my education that this lack, the absence of women writers, was never regarded as an issue. But then, there were perhaps more urgent matters to contend with – not least, racial discrimination and poverty. The fault, of course, could always be mine. Perhaps I did not take Minazana Dana seriously, even though I loved her words, the way she wrote, and the things she wrote about. I likely thought it too familiar, and therefore – like me – of little worth. How little I thought of myself, and of things specifically 'me'. I had definitely swallowed the apartheid lie – hook, line, and sinker! Did I recall Dana, use her as a resource, when I started teaching? Certainly not!

Vaguely recalled, also from my youth, there was Noni Jabavu.[9] Well, look whose daughter she was![10] Do you see my father, who did not complete primary school, fathering a writer then? Most unlikely, you might say. Noni Jabavu was as much a role model for me as any of the African male writers. They were very well educated – as was she. While she went off and obtained university degrees, I did not even have a matric certificate when I started working and had no hope of ever achieving that lofty standard of education. She may well have played a bigger role in my development, had I had the proper guidance.

My awakening was destined to be a gradual one. And, ironically, it was the very oppression that had moulded me into a person of so little faith in her own abilities that proved to be the instrument of my deliverance.

After I was abandoned by my husband, I could not forget the memory of my parents' sacrifice, and it was the recollection of their dream for me, contrasted with what I could see becoming of my own children that set me on the path to self-awareness. My children's downward trajectory contradicted my belief that each generation should achieve a better standard of living than the one before. At the rate things were going, if I was busy scrubbing floors in white homes, they would end up with less even than the pitiful education my parents had given me.

It is not supposed to be this way, screamed my wounded heart.

Then a gift from heaven fell onto my hands. Stella Petersen, a coloured high-school teacher, had befriended me. When she went to the United States on sabbatical, I was disappointed at the gift I received from her. But little did I know that Maya Angelou's *I Know Why the Caged Bird Sings* would be the key to my understanding of myself, and daring to imagine myself a writer.

Today I claim Maya Angelou as my mother. She tells of a 16-year-old leaving her mother's house, a baby in her arms, going off to make her own life. She birthed me – as a woman, but also as a single parent. She birthed me, too, as a writer. Black. Female. No university education. And Stella's book, a gift I had initially frowned upon in disdain, marked a turning point in my life. Of course, the writing bit would take ages in coming. But the picking oneself up from the dusty ground and brushing oneself off … that, I got. And there would be no going back!

What followed my enmeshment with Maya Angelou were introductions to other mentors such as Alice Walker and Toni Morrison – and, nearer to home, Ama Ata Aidoo, Buchi Emecheta, Mariama Bâ, and, later, Tsitsi Dangarembga and Véronique Tadjo. Through the works of these women I gradually came to see the oneness of womankind. The struggles they portrayed were familiar to me. Notably, I steered away from South African writers. I took the decision to stay away from writing by unique, special women of my country. Petty? Wrongheaded? Stupid, irrational, ignorant? The truth is, I was afraid that, in trying my hand at writing, I might unintentionally regurgitate their work. While I have never been accused of having a mirror-like memory, many are the faces self-sabotage wears, and cowardice is one I know only too well. The further away from home, even leaving Africa and reading US and South American writers, the more I realised that writers are, paradoxically, different and identical. For each book is nothing but an expression of the personhood of an author, and no two would ever produce identical books. All these women, in different ways, encouraged me to write my story because they spoke of worlds I understood – the world of womanhood, with all its ups and downs, its deprivations, its humiliations … and its enduring courage.

It would be disingenuous for me to say that there were not others who had a role in my making, who were, like André Brink, heroes rather than s/heroes. George Orwell helped spur my love of speculative dystopian fiction. And a writer such as Steve Biko really got to me: in *I Write What I Like*, Biko creates the kind of tension I also admire in speculative works. Alan Paton told a story I knew and understood; the marvel for me was that it was so widely celebrated and applauded. What did I know then of technique? Or the difference between fact and fiction, and narrative technique? Eventually, as I gained confidence in my own writing, in its authenticity, I dared read South African women writers – my fear of mirroring them had miraculously disappeared! Then, alert to my stupidity, I avidly devoured Lauretta Ngcobo's *And They Didn't Die* as well as her *Cross of God*; Miriam Tlali's *Muriel at Metropolitan*; and Nadine Gordimer's *July's People*.

Of late, either because I am getting on in years or because the situation in the country is growing more and more alarming, I seem to go back to lessons learnt from the writers of my growing years – men, mostly, of the same language group as I, amaXhosa. S.E.K. Mqhayi, A.C. Jordan and J.J.R. Jolobe come to mind. There were also prominent writers from the continent, my continent, Africa, Chinua Achebe foremost among these.

I need to put in a special word for Samuel Krune Mqhayi. His importance to me can be seen in the reflective essay that forms part of my PhD thesis. I was both excited and concerned that he featured so prominently, pleased that he had resurfaced from the depths of memory, coming to my aid. However, it bothered me that it was not a woman's name that had come to mind. Then

I reminded myself that this is partly why I – a woman – write, and will continue to write till I can do so no more. I reminded myself of the pledge I had made as a new writer, that I would write for as long as I lived, and write whatever came to me and knocked at the door of my heart, demanding entry. For then, I believe, I will be answering a call, with the Universe guiding me. So, when Mqhayi answered my call, I did not waver! There is a possibility that a chapter in my thesis, 'A Conversation with Mqhayi' will be published – which, for me, is hugely affirming.

Mqhayi was hailed as a poet, perhaps the greatest that ever voiced his thoughts in our beloved language, isiXhosa. All his work, but particularly *uDon Jadu* (*Don Jadu*), was written with the express purpose of gaining understanding and responding to the crisis of a changing society. Mqhayi wrote for his people, amaXhosa, and for other people of colour in the sub-region. He gave us what is today hailed as 'sociological thought', using his knowledge of what it meant to be a human being, a Christian, and a man of standing, particularly in his time, a time of momentous upheaval and disruption as a consequence of colonisation. He urged Africans to take great care regarding what the west brought to Africa. This new knowledge had to be appraised and evaluated, and only when found to be beneficial, should it be embraced. He sternly cautioned against doing so willy-nilly, and, even more sternly, against embracing the new at the expense of the old. What I applaud in his philosophy is the reasoning that tradition is time-linked, and when something is seen to have outlived its usefulness or become detrimental to the standards of the day, it should be discontinued. This is an important reminder to those controlling the discourse of post-apartheid black-black thinking who are frequently opposed to any change to, or adaptation of, tradition, as though it were God-given, even when it promotes sexism, oppression and the blatant abuse of women.

It has been said that we stand on the shoulders of giants, and although this is true of various endeavours in life, it is perhaps most true of writing, for in this specific pursuit, the only instruments are words and imagination. Those, and the pure heart of the writer, her intention to serve in her own particular manner, while walking in the footsteps of those who went before her. She treads lightly, though, for the road has been paved for her. Her antecedents had trod that road, and they now stand with her as she skips along; with firm, yet light and loving hands, they help her negotiate their stepping stones. Doing the work they had so dauntlessly done before her, leaving her own mark, she now hopes and prays she might one day join that august company of wordsmiths, guiding the next cohort as they take their first tentative steps, bridging Before and After in a continuum of service.

Having traced the footsteps of my honoured ancestors in my own little writer's world, it is necessary to emphasise that the acknowledgments here represent only a partial list of the many people who have influenced me. The homage I pay is but part of the debt I owe them. That debt can only be discharged by going on and on with my writing, and to do so is my heartfelt hope.

Camagu! [11]

NOTES

Foreword

1 Renée Schatteman, 'At This Time and in This Place: Renée Schatteman in Conversation with Sindiwe Magona', *New Contrast* 184, vol. 46 (Summer 2018): 5.
2 Schatteman, 'At This Time and in This Place': 9.
3 *Rediscovery of the Ordinary: Essays on South African Literature and Culture* (Johannesburg: COSAW, 1991) was also published under the title *South African Literature and Culture: Rediscovery of the Ordinary* (Manchester: Manchester University Press, 1994).
4 Ndebele, *South African Literature and Culture*, 24.
5 Ndebele, *South African Literature and Culture*, 24.
6 Linda Tuhiwai Smith, *Decolonizing Methodologies: Research and Indigenous Peoples* (London: Zed Books, 2012), 79.
7 Smith, *Decolonizing Methodologies*, 80.
8 Dianne Shober, 'Ecofeminist Invitations in the Works of Sindiwe Magona', *Literator* 38, no. 1 (2017): 2.

Introduction: Writing South Africa's Yawning Void

1 Sindiwe Magona, 'Statement', in *Please, Take Photographs* (Cape Town: Modjaji, 2009), 59
2 Sidney Zola Skweyiva, a South African politician, was Minister of Public Service and Administration from 1994 to 1999; Minister of Social Development from 1999 to 2009; and South African High Commissioner to the United Kingdom and Northern Ireland from 2009 to 2014.

Chapter 1: The Scars of Umlungu

1   *Umlungu* means white person in isiXhosa.
2   *Makhulu* means grandmother in isiXhosa.
3   Dongas are steep-sided gullies, usually created by water erosion.
4   Chloasma is a skin condition characterised by skin discoloration, particularly dark patches of skin.

Chapter 2: Clawing at Stones

1   Sindiwe Magona, 'Fear of Change', in *Please, Take Photographs* (Cape Town: Modjaji, 2009), 24.
2   Countrymeters, Africa, accessed 24 January 2023, https://countrymeters.info/en/Africa.
3   Albert Luthuli served as president of the ANC from 1952 to 1960; he was the first African to be awarded the Nobel Peace Prize for his commitment to non-violent protest as the necessary response to extreme racial discrimination. Reports stated that he was killed by a goods train while walking over a railway bridge, but many believe that this was no accident.
4   Steve Biko was a leading figure in the creation of the South African Students' Organisation (SASO) in 1969, and he was at the forefront of the Black Consciousness Movement of the 1960s and 1970s. The ideology behind this movement, which encouraged black autonomy and self-worth, was perceived as a threat to the apartheid regime; on 12 September 1977, Biko died from injuries inflicted on him while in police detention.
5   The literal meaning is Once, it happened, according to a tale! (loosely translated as Once upon a time …).
6   *Chosi!* is an isiXhosa exclamation meaning Well! (that is, may everything go as well as you hope it will).
7   An abbreviated version of the poem 'Mine Boys' appears in *Please, Take Photographs*, 27–28.
8   From the poem 'Penrose' in Magona's unpublished biography of her parents, Penrose and Lilian.

Chapter 3: Finding My Way Home

1   *Ndlovu* is isiXhosa for 'shepherd' and is also a clan name; '*A Ndlovu!*' is a salute.
2   A tribute in isiXhosa, meaning You, Miss Mabija, were a true shepherd – I thank you!
3   Karina Magdalena Szczurek, 'Beauty's Gift', *Itch*, 30 September 2008, accessed 22 January 2023, https://www.itch.co.za/archive/issue-2/item/135-beautys-gift.

Chapter 4: It is in the Blood: Trauma and Memory in the South African Novel

1 Lexicon Publications. *The New Lexicon Webster's Dictionary of the English Language* (New York: Lexicon, 1990), 1050.

2 *Isegazini* is an isiXhosa saying that means 'It is in the blood'.

3 Sindiwe Magona, 'Please, Take Photographs' in *Please, Take Photographs* (Cape Town: Modjaji, 2009), 45.

4 'South African Family in Crisis: SAIRR', *Times LIVE*, 4 April 2011, accessed 19 January 2023, https://www.timeslive.co.za/news/south-africa/2011-04-04-south-african-family-in-crisis-sairr/.

5 Mandla Langa was invited to the Conference on Trauma, Memory, and Narrative in the Contemporary South African Novel but had to cancel his participation at short notice. He was so kind as to send us his paper, which was read on his behalf by Yazir Henry.

6 *Iintsomi* means folktales in isiXhosa.

7 André Brink, *A Dry White Season* (London: Vintage 2000), 302.

8 Brink, *A Dry White Season*, 304.

9 Brink, *A Dry White Season*, 304.

10 Sindiwe Magona, *Mother to Mother* (Cape Town: David Philip, 1998), 3.

11 Magona, *Mother to Mother*, 210.

12 Magona, *Mother to Mother*, 210.

Chapter 5: Address at the Funeral of a Young Woman

1 This is no unusual occurrence.

2 Aids is colloquially known as 'The Chopper' because, like an axe, it strikes suddenly, and the blow can be fatal.

3 *Ubuntu* is a term in isiXhosa and isiZulu denoting compassion and humanity towards others.

4 *Iintloni* means a sense of shame in isiXhosa.

5 *Intlonipho* means a respectful manner in isiXhosa.

6 *Rha-haa* is an isiXhosa expression of disgust, equivalent to Ugh!

7 *Sies* is an Afrikaans expression that conveys disgust.

8 *Finish en klaar* is a colloquialism using a mixture of English and Afrikaans, which loosely translates as 'End of story! Nothing more to be said!'

9 *Amaqgwirha* means wizards/witches in isiXhosa.

10 IsiXhosa for 'If you don't want to continue suffering, let the whole world know about it'.

11 *Iqwili* is a vegetable root that the Xhosa people use for medicinal purposes, mainly to cure coughs.

Chapter 6: Do Not Choose Poverty

1 Black-black is a commonly-used term in South Africa to describe people who were classified Bantu (people) under apartheid.

2 *Dompas* is a derisive Afrikaans term for the hated pass book, literally 'stupid pass'.

3 Bantu is a term relating broadly to sub-Saharan Africans, which in isiXhosa and isiZulu means people; it was appropriated by the apartheid government. Today the preferred terms are Africans or black people.

4 Nusas was an anti-apartheid student organisation that promoted non-racialism.

5 Herschel Girls School, located in Cape Town, is a prestigious school that has long dedicated itself to empowering women.

6 *Foeitog* is an Afrikaans term expressing pity, as with a charity case.

Chapter 7: Cry, the Beloved Language

1 Alan Paton, *Cry, the Beloved Country: A Story of Comfort in Desolation* (London: Jonathan Cape, 1948). The year the book was first published was the year the newly-elected National Party introduced apartheid legislation.

2 This address was delivered at the 'Reclaiming African Heritage through Identity' conference of the African Language Association of Southern African, hosted by Walter Sisulu University in South Africa in 2014.

3 *NgamaXhosa* means by Xhosa people in isiXhosa.

4 NB Publishers is today the largest local publishing company in South Africa, and it has seven main imprints.

5 Chris Barnard performed the world's first human heart transplant operation; his brother Marius, also a cardiac surgeon, was part of his brother's team, and he also came up with the concept of critical illness insurance.

6 *Stokvel* is an Afrikaans word for an informal savings club whose (usually black) members draw funds on a rotational basis.

7 This means The land is dying while we watch.

8 *Ihlazo* means disgrace and *inyala* means abomination in isiXhosa.

9 This means What do you think you're doing? in isiXhosa.

10 Questions in isiXhosa expressing outrage that an abomination could happen in plain view: 'Where is everybody? Where was everybody?'

11 Mazisi Kunene (1930–2006) was an anti-apartheid activist and South African poet best known for compiling and translating the epic Zulu poem *Emperor Shaka*

the Great. In 1993 he was appointed Africa's first poet laureate by Unesco, and in 2005 he become South Africa's first poet laureate.

12 Herbert Isaac Ernest Dhlomo (1903–1956) was one of the founding figures of South African literature. His output included poems, short stories and plays, including *The Girl Who Killed to Save* (which deals with Nongqawuse and the Xhosa cattle killing tragedy of 1856–1857). His brother R.R.R. Dhlomo (1901–1971) was a journalist and writer best known for novels in isiZulu, including historical novels about Zulu kings, and *An African Tragedy*, the first novel written in English by a Zulu writer.

13 S.E.K. Mqhayi (1875–1945) was a Xhosa dramatist, essayist, critic, novelist, historian, biographer, translator and poet, who was a major influence on Sindiwe Magona's own thinking and writing.

14 A.C. Jordan (1906–1968) was a Xhosa novelist who lectured in Bantu languages and African studies at the University of Cape Town before leaving in 1961 to take up a post in the USA. His masterly novel *Ingqumbo Yeminyanya* (*The Wrath of the Ancestors*) examines the conflict between western education and traditional beliefs.

Chapter 8: We Are All Racists!

1 A location or township is a designated area on the outskirts of an urban area, where the apartheid government permitted people designated 'Bantu' to live. Following the forced removals of the late 1950s and early 1960s, Retreat was established near Cape Town.

2 Expression in IsiXhosa of anger and disgust: 'These Boer dogs!'

3 *Umphako* is food in isiXhosa; the travellers shared their leftovers with our grateful family.

4 Sven Lindquist, *Exterminate All the Brutes*, tr. Joan Tate (New York: The New Press, 1996).

5 *Sizenza abelungu* literally means making ourselves white (in other words, behaving like whites) in isiXhosa.

6 Robin DiAngelo, *White Fragility: Why It's So Hard for White People to Talk about Racism* (Boston: Beacon Press, 2018).

7 Kaffir (the 'K-word') is a deeply offensive racial slur, a serious form of *crimen injuria*. Its original meaning is 'unbeliever'.

Chapter 9: Why I Wrote My Autobiographies

1 The first such legislation, The Industrial Conciliation Act, was passed in 1924. This was followed by a plethora of similar laws, including the Mines and Works Act (Colour Bar Act) of 1926.

2 *Ixhwele* means medicine man in isiXhosa.

Chapter 10: Why I Wrote *Mother to Mother*

1 *Bangbroek* is an Afrikaans slang term meaning scaredy cat.

2 The Amy Biehl Foundation offers multiple programmes, including life skills, vocational skills training and sports, which develop and empower young people from vulnerable communities.

3 This is a fictitious name; in such cases I avoided using real names so as to protect the privacy of the individual concerned.

Chapter 11: Why I Wrote *Beauty's Gift*

1 *Sisi* is a term of respect in isiXhosa, used to address a woman slightly older than oneself.

Chapter 12: Why I Wrote *Chasing the Tails of My Father's Cattle*

1 *Oobhuti bethu* means our older brothers in isiXhosa.

2 *Tata* means father in isiXhosa.

3 The saying refers to a man who is useless in his role as father and husband. More educated African men wore hats at the time, and so a hat was a mark of being a grown man. But when a man failed in his duties, such as supporting his family, he was effectively 'dead'.

4 S.E.K. Mqhayi, National Poet Laureate of amaXhosa (1875–1945) was the author of respected works such as *Ityala Lamawele* (The Lawsuit of the Twins) and *UDon Jadu* (Don Jadu).

5 This means Please, look after my baby in isiXhosa.

6 Lobola is an African custom whereby a bridegroom's family makes a payment, usually in cattle, to the bride's family before the actual marriage ceremony.

7 *Indla-lifa* means the inheritor in isiXhosa.

8 *Ukutheleka* means the taking back of a man's wife by her own family; this might, for example, occur as a result of maltreatment of the wife.

9 *Chosi* is an exclamation meaning May it be so! in isiXhosa.

10 A warning that means Cowards, hearken, the enemy are stealing away with our cattle! in isiXhosa.

Chapter 13: Why I Wrote *When the Village Sleeps*

1 The *False Bay Echo* is a community newspaper in the southern suburbs of Cape Town. We tried to contact the paper to ask for the citation to the article, but were unsuccessful.

2 Jake McKinstry, 'Using the Past to Step Forward: Fetal Alcohol Syndrome in the Western Cape Province of South Africa', *American Journal of Public Health* 95, no. 7 (July 2005): 1097–1099.

3 The needs-based Child Support Grant programme was introduced in 1998, providing eligible parents or guardians with a monthly grant for each child.

4 *Umbheka-phesheya* is a traditional long-stemmed pipe with a beaded-handle used by Xhosa women.

5 *Umqombothi* is a traditional beer brewed by Xhosa women, using maize, sorghum and yeast/fermentation.

6 This is translated in *The Lawsuit of the Twins* as follows: 'It is the adult's place/duty that, whether at home or a traveller along the way, that adult remonstrate, warn, scold or even punish any child s/he sees doing what is not right/wrong; irrespective of whether or not the child is known to him/her. It is a danger to him/her [the adult] to say nothing, for their eyes or ears have already brought them obligation/responsibility'. *The Lawsuit of the Twins*, (Oxford: Oxford University Press, 2019, 107.

7 This means balding begins with the slow receding of the hairline in isiXhosa.

8 A.C. Jordan (1906–1968), a Xhosa novelist, lectured in Bantu languages and African studies at the University of Cape Town. His novel *Ingqumbo Yezinyanya* (*The Wrath of the Ancestors*), which is considered a masterpiece of Xhosa writing, examines the conflict between western education and traditional beliefs.

9 *Mpundulu* means firebird in isiXhosa.

10 A.C. Jordan, *The Wrath of the Ancestors* (Johannesburg: Ad Donker, 2004).

11 A saying in isiXhosa that roughly translates as 'You snooze, you lose!'

12 SASSA issues the Child Support Grant to eligible parents or guardians.

13 *Gogga*, or insect, is an Afrikaans term of endearment, though here it also hints at the child's abnormalities.

Chapter 14: Why I Write Children's Stories

1 *Makhulu* means grandma in isiXhosa.

2 Loosely translated, this means Once upon a time … in isiXhosa.

3 Sindiwe Magona and Nina G. Jablonski, *Skin We Are In: A Celebration of the Evolution of Skin Colour*, illustrated by Lynn Fellman (Cape Town: David Philip, 2018). This book was adapted for the stage in 2023.

4 Established in 1997 at Stellenbosch University, STIAS supports experts who work across disciplinary borders to tackle difficult problems through innovative thinking and creative strategies.

5 Bridget Kahts, Claire Pearce and Eric Atmore, eds. *Madiba: Our Children's Champion* (Lansdowne: Centre for Early Childhood Development, 2022).

6 Madiba is the clan name of the Mandela family; it is often used as a mark of respect – and affection – for Nelson Mandela.

7   Annika Forsberg Langa, 'Fought for all Children', The World's Children's Prize, accessed 23 January 2023, https://worldschildrensprize.org/nelsonmandela.

8   Nelson Mandela, 'Speech by President Nelson Mandela at the launch of the Nelson Mandela Children's Fund, 8 May 1995', Office of the President, accessed 22 January 2023, http://www.mandela.gov.za/mandela_speeches/1995/950508_nmcf.htm.

Conclusion: A Tribute to Those Who Came Before Me

1   The Franschhoek Literary Festival is an annual event, held in Franschhoek in the Western Cape.

2   André Brink died on 6 February 2015.

3   Claremont is a suburb of Cape Town.

4   A phrase in French meaning That's life, isn't it?

5   The Sestigers ('Sixtiers' or writers of the sixties) were a group of young Afrikaner novelists who had studied abroad in the 1960s, whose innovative writings broke with the past.

6   Loosely translated, this saying in isiXhosa means We ask those who have gone before us where the buck may be found.

7   This means A mighty tree has fallen in isiXhosa.

8   *UmXhosakazi* means a Xhosa woman in isiXhosa.

9   Noni Jabavu (1919–2008), one of the first African women to pursue a literary career, is known for her journalism and her autobiographical writings.

10 D.D.T Jabavu, the father of Noni Jabavu, was a professor at the University of Fort Hare, as well as a journalist and activist.

11 *Camagu!* means May the Ancestors agree! in isiXhosa.

SELECTED WORKS

Non-fiction

To My Children's Children (autobiography). Cape Town: David Philip, 1990.

Kubantwana Babantwana Bam (autobiography, transl. *To My Children's Children*). Cape Town: New Africa Books, 1995.

Forced To Grow (autobiography). Cape Town: David Philip, 1992.

From Robben Island to Bishopscourt: The Biography of Archbishop Njongonkulu Ndungane. Cape Town: New Africa Books, 2011.

With Beverly Kirsch and Silvia Skorge. *Teach Yourself Xhosa: A Complete Course in Understanding, Speaking and Writing* (kit). Johannesburg: Hodder and Stoughton, 2000.

With Beverley Kirsch and Sylvia Skorge. *Clicking with Xhosa: A Xhosa Phrasebook.* Cape Town: David Philip, 2001.

With Thembi Mtshali-Jones. *Theatre Road: My Story As Told to Sindiwe Magona.* Cape Town: Karavan Press, 2019.

Fiction

Living, Loving and Lying Awake at Night and Other Stories. Cape Town: David Philip, 1991.

Push-Push! and Other Stories. Cape Town: David Philip, 1996.

Mother To Mother. Cape Town: David Philip, 1998.

'A State of Outrage'. In *Opening Spaces:* An Anthology of Contemporary African Women's Writing, edited by Yvonne Vera, 114–127. Harare: Baobab, 1999.

'Leave-Taking'. In *Nobody Ever Said AIDS: Stories and Poems from Southern Africa*, compiled and edited by Nobantu Rasebotsa, Meg Samuelson and Kylie Thomas, 124–141. Cape Town: Kwela Books, 2005.

'Modi's Bride'. In *African Love Stories: An Anthology*, edited by Ama Ata Aidoo, 135–148. Banbury: Ayebia Clarke, 2006.

Co-edited with Petra Muller. *Twist: Short Stories Inspired by Tabloid Headlines*. Cape Town: Oshun Books, 2006.

Beauty's Gift. Cape Town: Kwela Books, 2008.

Chasing the Tails of My Father's Cattle. Cape Town: Seriti Sa Sechaba Publishers, 2015.

When the Village Sleeps. Johannesburg: Picador Africa, 2021.

Plays

Vukani! Wake Up! Cape Town: Juta Gariep, 2007.

Poetry

Please, Take Photographs. Cape Town: Modjaji Books, 2009.

Children's and Young Adult Fiction

Many of the works listed here are also available in other languages.

With Dianne Stewart and Jude Daly. *Ihobe*. Pietermaritzburg: Songololo Books, 1994.

Bunzima nje Buhle Ubomi!/Life is a Hard but Beautiful Thing! Cape Town: Juta Gariep, 2005.

Esona Sona Sidlo!/The Best Meal Ever!/Die Heel, Heel Lekkerste Kos! Cape Town: Tafelberg, 2006.

Imida: Incwadi Yezincoko. Cape Town: Realities Xhosa, 2006.

With Vusi Malindi and Nonikiwe Mashologu. *Nkanishe Motho Ya Manganga*. Pretoria: Room to Read South Africa, 2008.

Awam Ngqo! Cape Town: Juta Gariep, 2009.

Sigalelekile (series, 48 storybooks). Cape Town: Via Afrika, 2009.

With Gcina Mhlope. *Siyakhula/We Are Growing* (series, 89 storybooks). Cape Town: Oxford University Press, 2009.

With H.C. Andersen. *UDadana Ombi* [The Ugly Duckling]. Johannesburg: Jacana Media, 2010.

African Folk Tales (series, 18 storybooks). Cape Town: David Philip Publishers, 2014.

Books and Bricks at Manyano School. Cape Town: David Philip Publishers, 2014.

With Ellen Mayer. *Books and Bricks: How a School Rebuilt the Community*. Cambridge, MA: Star Bright Books, 2017.

With Elinor Sisulu. *Albertina Sisulu*. Cape Town: David Philip, 2018.

With Nina Jablonski. *Skin We Are In*. Cape Town: David Philip, 2018.

With Sinomonde Ngwane and Thulisizwe Mamba. *Palesa Can Walk!* Cape Town: Book Dash, 2018.

With Nicolene Louw. *Woof-Woof!* Cape Town: Book Dash, 2019.

Essays

'The Scars of Umlungu'. *New Internationalist* 230 (April 1992): 8–9.

'South Africa's Curse'. *New York Times*, 4 August 1998: Section A, 13.

'Clawing at Stones'. In *The Spirit of Writing: Classic and Contemporary Essays Celebrating the Writing Life*, edited by Mark Waldman, 7–13. New York: Penguin, 2001.

'With a Heavy Heart, I Watched Freedom Come'. In *Freedom Spring: Ten Years On: A Celebration and Commemoration of Ten Years of Freedom in South Africa*, edited by Suhayl Saadi and Catherine McInerney, 56–63. Glasgow: Waverly Books, 2005.

'Home'. In *A City Imagined*, edited by Stephen Watson, 107–116. Cape Town: Penguin, 2006.

'It is in the Blood: Trauma and Memory in the South African Novel'. In *Trauma, Memory, and Narrative in the Contemporary South African Novel*, edited by Ewald Mengel and Michela Borzaga, 93–105. Amsterdam: Rodopi, 2012.

'Why I Wrote *Beauty's Gift*'. Introduction to *Mother to Mother*, Cape Town: Pan Macmillan, 2018, 1–39.

'Why I Wrote my Autobiographies'. *Five Points* 19, no. 1 (Winter 2018): 102–106.

'On Writing from a Postcolonial Perspective'. Oxford Research Encyclopedias: Literature, 29 November 2021. Accessed 20 January 2023. https://doi.org/10.1093/acrefore/9780190201098.013.1285.

BIBLIOGRAPHY

Achebe, Chinua. *Things Fall Apart*. London, Penguin Classics, 2006 [1958].

Angelou, Maya. *I Know Why the Caged Bird Sings*. New York: Random House, 2009 [1969].

Biko, Steve. *I Write What I Like: Selected Writings*. Johannesburg: Picador Africa, 2004 [1978].

Brink, André. *A Dry White Season*. London: Vintage, 2000 [1979].

Dana, Minazana. *Kufundwa Ngamava*. Oxford: Oxford University Press, 1990 [1963].

Dhlomo, H.I.E. *The Girl Who Killed to Save (Nongqawuse the Liberator)*. In *H.I.E. Dhlomo Collected Works*, edited by Tim Couzens and Nic Visser, 3–29. Johannesburg: Ravan Press, 1985 [1935].

Dhlomo, H.I.E. *Cetshwayo*. Alexandria, VA: Alexander Street Press, 2003 [1936–1937].

Dhlomo, R.R.R. *An African Tragedy*. Alice: Lovedale Press, 1928.

DiAngelo, Robin. *White Fragility: Why It's So Hard for White People to Talk about Racism*. Boston: Beacon Press, 2018.

Gordimer, Nadine. *July's People*. London: Jonathan Cape, 1981.

Gqola, Pumla Dineo. *What is Slavery to Me? Postcolonial/Slave Memory in Post-Apartheid South Africa*. Johannesburg: Wits University Press, 2010.

Gqola, Pumla Dineo. *Rape: A South African Nightmare*. Johannesburg: Jacana Media, 2015.

Gqola, Pumla Dineo. *Reflecting Rogue: Inside the Mind of a Feminist*. Johannesburg: Jacana Media, 2018.

Gqola, Pumla Dineo. *Female Fear Factory: Unravelling Patriarchy's Cultures of Violence*. London: Cassava Republic, 2021.

Haffajee, Ferial. *What If There Were No Whites in South Africa?* Johannesburg: Picador Africa, 2015.

Jabavu, Noni. *Drawn in Colour*. London: John Murray, 1960.

Jabavu, Noni. *The Ochre People*. London: John Murray, 1963.

Jordan, A.C. *Ingqumbo Yeminyanya*. Alice, South Africa: Lovedale Press, 1940.

Jordan, A.C. *The Wrath of the Ancestors*. Johannesburg, Ad Donker, 2004.

Kahts, Bridget, Claire Pearce and Eric Atmore, eds. *Madiba: Our Children's Champion*. Lansdowne: Centre for Early Childhood Development, 2022.

Kunene, Mazisi. *Emperor Shaka the Great*. Pietermaritzburg: University of KwaZulu-Natal Press, 2017 [1979].

Langa, Annika Forsberg. 'Fought for all Children'. The World's Children's Prize. Accessed 23 Jaunary 2023. https://worldschildrensprize.org/nelsonmandela.

Lindquist, Sven. *Exterminate All the Brutes!* Translated by Joan Tate. New York: The New Press, 1996.

Magona, Sindiwe. *To My Children's Children*. Cape Town: David Philip, 1990.

Magona, Sindiwe. *Living, Loving and Lying Awake at Night*. Cape Town: David Philip, 1991.

Magona, Sindiwe. *Forced to Grow*. Cape Town: David Philip, 1992.

Magona, Sindiwe. 'The Scars of Umlungu'. *New Internationalist* 230 (April 1992): 8–9.

Magona, Sindiwe. *Push-Push! and Other Stories*. Cape Town: David Philip, 1996.

Magona, Sindiwe. *Mother to Mother*. Cape Town: David Philip, 1998.

Magona, Sindiwe. 'Clawing at Stones'. In *The Spirit of Writing: Classic and Contemporary Essays Celebrating the Writing Life*, edited by Mark Waldman. New York: Penguin, 2001, 7–13.

Magona, Sindiwe. 'Finding My Way Home'. *Fairlady* (June 2006): 57.

Magona, Sindiwe. *Beauty's Gift*. Cape Town: Kwela Books, 2008.

Magona, Sindiwe. *Please, Take Photographs*. Cape Town: Modjaji Books, 2009.

Magona, Sindiwe. *Vukani! (Wake Up!)*. In *African Women Playwrights*, compiled and edited by Kathy Perkins, 170–221. Champaign, IL: University of Illinois Press, 2009.

Magona, Sindiwe. 'It is in the Blood: Trauma and Memory in the South African Novel'. In *Trauma, Memory and Narrative in the Contemporary South African Novel*, edited by Ewald Mengal and Michela Borzaga, 93–105. Amsterdam: Rodopi, 2012.

Magona, Sindiwe. *Chasing the Tails of My Father's Cattle*. Cape Town: Seriti sa Sechaba Publishers, 2015.

Magona, Sindiwe. 'The Impact of Colonialism & Postcolonialism on Women's Writing'. *Five Points: A Journal of Literature and Art* 19, no. 1 (2018): 102–106.

Magona, Sindiwe. 'Why I Wrote *Beauty's Gift*'. Introduction to *Beauty's Gift*. Cape Town: Pan Macmillan, 2018, 1–39.

Magona, Sindiwe. *When the Village Sleeps*. Johannesburg: Picador Africa, 2021.

Magona, Sindiwe and Nina G. Jablonski. *Skin We Are In: A Celebration of the Evolution of Skin Colour*. Illustrated by Lynn Fellman. Cape Town: David Philip, 2018.

Magubane, Peter. *Magubane's South Africa*. London: Random House, 2019 [1978].

Mandela, Nelson. 'Speech by President Nelson Mandela at the launch of the Nelson Mandela Children's Fund, 8 May 1995'. Office of the President. Accessed 22 January 2023. http://www.mandela.gov.za/mandela_speeches/1995/950508_nmcf.htm.

McCallum, Ian. *Ecological Intelligence. Rediscovering Ourselves in Nature*. Wheat Ridge, CO: Fulcrum Publishing, 2008.

McKinstry, Jake. 'Using the Past to Step Forward: Fetal Alchohol Syndrome in the Western Cape Province of SA'. *American Journal of Public Health* 95, no. 7 (July 2005): 1097–1099.

Ngcobo, Lauretta. *And They Didn't Die*. Johannesburg: Skotaville Publishers, 1990.

Mqhayi, S.E.K. *Ityala Lamawele*. Alice, South Africa: Lovedale Press, 1914.

Mqhayi, S.E.K. *Don Jadu*. Translated by T. Mabeqa, N. Mpolweni and T. Ntwana. Cape Town: Oxford University Press, 2018.

Mqhayi, S.E.K. *The Lawsuit of the Twins*. Translated by T. Mabeqa. Oxford: Oxford University Press, 2018.

Ndebele, Njabulo. *South African Literature and Culture: Rediscovery of the Ordinary*. Manchester: Manchester University Press, 1994 [1991].

Ndebele, Njabulo. *Fine Lines from the Box*. Cape Town: Umuzi, 2007.

Paton, Alan. *Cry, the Beloved Country: A Story of Comfort in Desolation*. London: Jonathan Cape, 1948.

Schatteman, Renée. 'At This Time and In This Place: Renée Schatteman in Conversation with Sindiwe Magona'. *New Contrast* 184, no. 46 (Summer 2018): 5–12.

Shober, Dianne. 'Ecofeminist Invitations in the Works of Sindiwe Magona'. *Literator: Journal of Literary Criticism, Comparative Linguistics, and Literary Studies* 38, no. 1 (2017): 1–10.

Smith, Linda Tuhiwai. *Decolonizing Methodologies: Research and Indigenous Peoples*. London: Zed Books, 2012 [1999].

Szczurek, Karina Magdalena. 'Beauty's Gift'. *Itch*, 30 September 2008. Accessed 22 January 2023. https://www.itch.co.za/archive/issue-2/item/135-beautys-gift.

Times LIVE. 'South African Family in Crisis: SAIRR'. 4 April 2011. Accessed 19 January 2023. https://www.timeslive.co.za/news/south-africa/2011-04-04-south-african-family-in-crisis-sairr/.

Tlali, Miriam. *Muriel at Metropolitan: A Novel*. Harlow: Longman, 1987 [1975].

Wicomb, Zoë. *David's Story*. New York: The Feminist Press at CUNY, 2000.

Wicomb, Zoë. *Playing in the Light*. New York: The New Press, 2006.

Wicomb, Zoë. *Race, Nation, Translation: South African Essays, 1990–2013*. New Haven: Yale University Press, 2018.

INDEX

CPSIA information can be obtained
at www.ICGtesting.com
Printed in the USA
JSHW020507060723
44257JS00006B/15

9 781776 148189